Introducing

'POWER FOR LIFE'

oOo

A Compilation of Twelve bestselling inspirational books

By
ROBERT W. WOOD D.HP
(Diploma in Hypnotherapy)

Rosewood Publishing

First Published in the U.K. 2013
By Rosewood Publishing
P.O. Box 219, Huddersfield,
West Yorkshire, HD2 2YT
UK

www.rosewood-gifts.co.uk

Robert W. Wood D.Hp
Asserts the moral right to be identified
as the Author of this work.

Copy-editing
Margaret Wakefield BA (Hons) London
www.euroreportage.co.uk

Cover designed by Robert W Wood D.Hp

Cover photograph by
Andrew Caveney BA (Hons)
www.creativedigitalphotography.co.uk

ISBN 978-0-9567913-3-7   BK14

'Power for Life'
introducing
a series of twelve inspirational books.

"For those who can enjoy that feeling of being connected, or are just curious about gemstones and crystals, astrology and birthstones, crystal dowsing and crystal healing then this 'Power for Life' series of twelve books could be ideal for you."

INTRODUCTION

It all seemed to have started with a chance meeting in a church. An event that at the time seemed to be quite insignificant; but over time has proved to have been quite a life changing occasion.

I was invited to a friend's daughter's confirmation. I can't remember how I came to have it – whether someone else had bought it, or whether I had – but I was wearing a small brooch in the shape of a fish, for the first time that day (14th March 1989). There are times in everybody's life when things happen that can change the direction of life for ever. What happened to me next was that kind of event.

The service had finished and the vicar had announced that coffee would be served at the back of the church.

We had not intended to stay for coffee. The church was really full, with my wife Moira we were sitting on the left hand side of the church, a third of the way down from the back. Moira said "Let's go, we don't really know anybody so let's go." But I had a 'feeling', "No", I said, wait a moment." Again Moira said, "Let's go," and started to get up. But I repeated, "Wait," and for some reason unknown to me I was getting annoyed with her for wanting to leave. "Wait," I said again, "something's going to happen. "My 'feeling, or intuition, told me that I had to wait.

So we sat there while the church slowly emptied. Then I said, "It's OK, we can go now," It was as if by magic; as if I was being directed, not by a voice but by a 'feeling'.

3

Moira just gave me a look as if I was mad.

We edged our way to the centre aisle, which was very busy, and as I was making my way to the back of the church and the way out, someone seemed to jump out in front of me saying, "Ah! I see another committed Christian."

I looked round to see who he was talking about – but what I hadn't realised was that he had seen my Christian brooch, in the sign of the fish, the one I was wearing for the very first time that day. I had always been a little scared to wear it in case somebody asked me about it. I had already had a few 'run-ins' with friends who knew I'd 'caught religion'.

This man introduced himself as Clinton, and told me he was starting a Christians in Business luncheon group, and that the very first meeting would be the following Wednesday. Rooms had been booked in a local hotel, and he would like to invite me to come.

Clinton owns a very large wholesale business supplying Gemstones, fossils and minerals as well as jewellery components to the trade – a very successful business, by any standards. I had never met him before, but my then business partner had, and I think this is how he knew that I might be interested. And although I didn't realise it at the time, during the recession of the 1980's, my business started to decline.

I have always been interested in sales and marketing and was fortunate enough to have been commissioned by Clintons Company to look into the idea of selling gemstones and crystals through 'party plan' and after several meetings came up with the idea of marketing

Birthstones as a 'theme'. After birthstones came extensive research into Healing crystals.

To help and support retailers to sell more gemstones and crystals I wrote a very simple mini-book on Birthstones and had five thousand copies printed. To everybody's surprise thousands sold and this encouraged me to write a second book, this time it was to help Alternative practitioners as well as retailers towards the esoteric values of combinations of stones.

And had the same success with the book, 'A Glossary of Healing stones, again thousands sold.

Then a third book, 'How to Create a Wish Kit' proved just as popular. To say I had 'caught the bug' was an understatement I was finding the mysteries that surrounded gemstones and crystals fascinating.

As a committed Christian I took a lot of 'stick' whenever I told anybody that I gave talks and wrote on the subject of gemstones and crystals including birthstones and healing crystals. You would have thought I had sold my soul to the devil especially if I had listened to some of my 'so called' Christian friends.

However it turned out that party plan was not that suitable for selling gemstones and crystals. One reason being you couldn't always get hold of certain gemstones and often the colour and quality varied too much. So I decided to take professional advice and it was suggested I continued to write a series of mini-books. I was already regularly giving talks to various ladies groups and so I decided to take a year out and then wrote a further nine books. Over 100,000 of these books are in print and can be seen on eBay and Amazon regularly.

The interesting thing about these books is that they start off with a simple guide book and then slowly as each one was written they became more conversational. Even stranger was the twelfth book 'Change your Life' I have often heard of song writers say that the words just came into their heads but never quite appreciated just what that meant until it happened to me. My twelfth book 'Change your Life' seemed to just write itself and is much more philosophical. "The most powerful crystal on earth can be yours".
Power for Life

This book is so disarmingly simple to understand; and yet contains within it a tremendous depth of knowledge.

So, from a chance meeting in a church; twelve mini-books have now been written. It's as if each book represents a chapter in a main book and fulfils my mission to 'de-mystify the mysteries. It's taken over twenty years of research to produce this book and now one other book has been written and is available, it's called 'An Alternative View on Crystal Healing' written by Robert W Wood D.Hp. Just search the web and you'll easily find it. Next comes a list of all twelve mini-books and then each book will be reproduced in the same running order, just as they were originally written.

All twelve titles in the 'POWER FOR LIFE' mini-series are listed here in the same running order just as they were written:-

BK1 ... Discover your own Special Birthstone and the renowned Healing Powers of Crystals... A look at Birthstones, personality traits and characteristics associated with each sign of the Zodiac – plus a guide to the author's own unique range of Power Gems.

BK2 ... A Special Glossary of Healing Stones plus Birthstones ... An introduction to Crystal Healing, with an invaluable Glossary listing common ailments and suggesting combinations of Gemstone and Crystals.

BK3 ... Create a Wish Kit using a Candle, a Crystal and the Imagination of your Mind ... 'The key to happiness is having dreams; the key to success is making dreams come true.' This book will help you to achieve.

BK4 ... 'Gemstone and Crystal Elixirs' – Potions for Love, Health, Wealth, Energy and Success ... An Ancient form of 'magic', invoking super-natural powers. You won't believe the power you can get from a drink!

BK5 ... Crystal Pendulum for Dowsing ... An ancient knowledge for unlocking your Psychic Power, to seek out information not easily available by any other means. Contains easy-to-follow instructions.

BK6 ... Crystal Healing – Fact or Fiction? Real or Imaginary? ... You can find an answer in this book. Discover a hidden code used by Jesus Christ for healing, and read about the science of light and colour. It's really amazing.

BK7 ... 'How to Activate the Hidden Power' in Gemstones and Crystals ... The key is to energise the thought by using a crystal. The conscious can direct – but discover the real power. It's all in this book.

BK8 … Astrology: The secret Code … In church it's called a 'Myers Briggs Typology'. In this book it's called 'psychological profiling'

BK9 … Talismans, Charms and Amulets … making possible the powerful transformations which we would no normally feel empowered to do without a little extra help. Learn how to make a lucky talisman.

BK10 … A Guide into the Mysteries Surrounding Gemstones and Crystals … Crystal healing, birthstones, crystal gazing, lucky talismans, elixirs, crystal dowsing, astrology, rune stones, amulets and rituals.

BK11 … A Simple Guide to Gemstone and Crystal Power – a mystical A-Z of stones … From an Agate to a Zircon, all you ever needed or wanted to know about the mystical powers of gemstones and crystals.

BK12 … Change Your Life by Using the Most Powerful Crystal on Earth … The most powerful crystal on earth can be yours. A book that is so disarmingly simple to understand. And yet has a tremendous depth of knowledge.

Also now available:-

BK13 … An Alternative View on Crystal Healing … What if it's not the crystal but the belief in the crystal. What if "it's all in the mind?" Wouldn't it be worth looking in the mind just in case? What if there's another avenue we haven't explored quite so well yet? This book explores not only Crystal Healing but an alternative idea to Crystal Healing based on 'belief.

Here's a question:-

Would you be impressed if I said, 'by using a touch of mystery, by revealing a 'Secret Formula', by showing you a deeply hidden essential ingredient, one that once it has been revealed and understood will change your life for the better and for ever,?

If I could de-mystify the mysteries and show you beyond any doubt, how to turn your Birthstone into a special powerful Lucky Talisman and at the same time show you how to get your Healing Crystal to become so effective that you will be amazed and astounded by its power.

If I told you that all this can be done by you, because you have a 'Power' that's beyond your imagination and then help you to discover it, and then go on to show you how to use it, well! Would you be impressed?

Because this is exactly what I have been doing, quietly and sincerely, for many years with the help of my talks and with stunning effect. So would you be impressed? Because that is exactly what the following books are all about.

"You are now invited to come along and read all twelve books completely in their original form starting with the first book written 'Discover your own special Birthstone'

Robert W. Wood D.Hp

Discover your own special

Birthstone

and

the renowned Healing Powers of

Crystals

By

Robert W. Wood D.Hp
(Diploma in Hypnotherapy)

Rosewood publishing

BK1

SIGNS of the ZODIAC

Awake to a glorious world of mystery.
By looking into your heart
you will find the truth, who you are,
what is right and what is not,
always remembering that beauty and
goodness exist in everything.

BIRTHSTONES

The Greeks gave us the now-familiar twelve signs of the Zodiac, but it was Carl Gustav Jung who, at the turn of the century, successfully linked his special form of psychology with astrology. He was interested to show how the collective and individual expressions of energy could be linked with the signs of the Zodiac.

It is a little known fact that, while your sun sign generally reflects your outward image, it would appear that your opposite sign reveals the true 'inner' you. Try it: first read your own star sign, and then read your opposite.

See if Jung is right!

ARIES
The Ram
Element: FIRE
Key Phrase:
I HAVE TO KNOW WHO I AM

21st Mar - 20th Apr   **Birthstone:**   **RED JASPER**
The First House (ruled by MARS)
Arians have a straightforward and positive attitude to life. They need adventure and like to take risks. They are passionate and sexy people but can be aggressive and dominating.
Positive traits: Courageous, enthusiastic, independent, forthright, active, energetic
Negative traits: Extravagant, impulsive, brash, selfish, impatient, headstrong

TAURUS
The Bull
Element: EARTH
Key Phrase:
I NEED TO SEE WHAT I AM

21st Apr - 21st May   **Birthstone:**   **ROSE QUARTZ**
The Second House (ruled by VENUS)
Taureans are very loyal, sensible and reliable, but need security and routine in their lives. They are passionate lovers but can be very possessive and stubborn.
Positive traits: Sincere, reliable, stable, faithful, solid, dependable
Negative traits: Obsessive, intransigent, possessive, naive, obstinate, plodding

GEMINI
The Twins
Element: AIR
Key Phrase:
I NEED TO KNOW WHAT I AM

22nd May - 21st Jun   **Birthstone:**   **BLACK ONYX**
The Third House (ruled by MERCURY)
Very chatty, lively people who make good salespeople, with a natural ability to sell. Geminis can be charming, flirty and fun, but can be impatient with others.
Positive traits: Humorous, communicative, ingenious, witty, versatile, spontaneous
Negative traits: Emotionally detached, inclined to exaggerate, flighty, restless, fickle

CANCER
The Crab
Element: WATER
Key Phrase:
I MUST KNOW MY ORIGINS

22nd Jun - 22nd Jul   **Birthstone:**   **MOTHER OF PEARL**
The Fourth House (ruled by the MOON)
Real Cancerians are very nice, caring and sensitive, with a tendency to worry. They can be moody but are very faithful and supportive to partners.

Positive traits: Industrious, thrifty, loyal, sympathetic, sensitive, tenacious
Negative traits: Secretive, capricious, cloying, over-emotional, touchy, clinging

LEO
The Lion
Element: FIRE
Key Phrase:
I AM CAPABLE OF BECOMING MORE

23rd Jul - 23rd Aug   **Birthstone:**   **TIGER EYE**
The Fifth House (ruled by the SUN)
Leos are leaders and organisers who love life. They are generous and like to spend money. They can be dominating and very vain, but can also be warm and enthusiastic.
Positive traits: Benevolent, hospitable, forgiving, affectionate, regal, magnanimous
Negative traits: Self-centred, uncompromising, vain, gullible, domineering

VIRGO
The Virgin
Element: EARTH
Key Phrase:
I MUST ALWAYS STRIVE FOR PERFECTION

24th Aug - 22nd Sep   **Birthstone:**   **CARNELIAN**
The Sixth House (ruled by MERCURY)
Virgoans are workers, practical and neat in every way. They can be perfectionists and critical of others. They are also very genuine people who tend to worry.
Positive traits: Painstaking, analytical, studious, considerate, discriminating
Negative traits: Self-effacing, prone to worry, detached, sceptical, cynical

LIBRA
The Scales
Element: AIR

Key Phrase:
I MUST JUSTIFY MY
EXISTENCE

23rd Sep - 23rd Oct   **Birthstone:**   **GREEN AVENTURINE**
The Seventh House (ruled by VENUS)
This is the sign of fair play and harmony. Librans are charmers who enjoy socialising and do not like to feel left out. They manage to appear calm in situations, but can be indecisive.
Positive traits: Gracious, cheerful, charming, refined, diplomatic
Negative traits: Manipulative, procrastinating, indecisive, impressionable

SCORPIO
The Scorpion
Element: WATER

Key Phrase:
I AM NOT ALONE

24th Oct - 22nd Nov   **Birthstone:**   **RHODONITE**
The Eighth House (ruled by MARS & PLUTO)
Scorpios are energetic, intense, sensual people. They enjoy positions of power and are very searching. They are secretive and jealous, with a tendency to be over-possessive with partners, but enjoy an active sexual relationship.
Positive traits: Resourceful, decisive, penetrating, persuasive, competitive, focused
Negative traits: Resentful, vindictive, sarcastic, jealous, suspicious, cunning

SAGITTARIUS
The Centaur
Element: FIRE

Key Phrase:
I LOVE TO LIVE

23rd Nov - 21st Dec   **Birthstone:**   **SODALITE**
The Ninth House (ruled by JUPITER)
Hunters, who need freedom and stimulation. Sagittarians are enthusiastic and fun-loving, with a thirst for knowledge. They need a lot of understanding as they can be unreliable and restless, especially within the confines of a relationship.
Positive traits: Frank, logical, kind, generous, optimistic, honest
Negative traits: Extravagant, quarrelsome, blunt, dictatorial, irresponsible

CAPRICORN
The Goat
Element: EARTH
Key Phrase:
NIL DESPERANDUM

22nd Dec - 20th Jan   **Birthstone:**   **OBSIDIAN SNOWFLAKE**
The Tenth House (ruled by SATURN)
Capricorns are ambitious, hard-working, independent individuals who enjoy good taste. They have a tendency to be bossy and stubborn, with a need for financial security and stability.
Positive traits: Profound, patient, practical, efficient, ambitious, hard-working
Negative traits: Gloomy, snobbish, materialistic, arrogant, intolerant, pessimistic

AQUARIUS
The Water Carrier
Element: AIR
Key Phrase:
I BELONG TO THE
FAMILY OF MAN

21st Jan - 19th Feb   **Birthstone:**   **BLUE ONYX**
The Eleventh House (ruled by SATURN & URANUS)
Aquarians make excellent friends as they are understanding and faithful. They are complex characters, original and magnetic. They can appear eccentric at times, and have lively traits.
Positive traits: Humane, trustworthy, caring, intuitive, friendly, broad-minded
Negative traits: Unpredictable, moody, rebellious, stubborn, abrupt, impersonal

PISCES
The Fish
Element: WATER
Key Phrase:
I WISH I COULD
COME BACK SOME
OTHER TIME

20th Feb - 20th Mar   **Birthstone:**   **AMETHYST**
The Twelfth House (ruled by JUPITER & NEPTUNE)
Pisceans are creative and imaginative but sometimes lack confidence. They are very caring, sensitive, kind characters. Lack of ambition is one of their negative traits, together with vagueness and indecision.
Positive traits: Unassuming, courteous, artistic, imaginative, gentle, lenient
Negative traits: Apologetic, irrational, changeable, self-pitying, hypersensitive

Is there   Hidden Power in Gemstones?
Judge for yourself!

The idea of being cured by a lump of rock may sound crazy, but it is said that precious gems have been doing that since the dawn of time.

Does it work? The only evidence is from the people who believe it does.

However, scientific research has shown an amazing fact: that each type of crystal vibrates at a different frequency. For example, a digital watch works because of a small piece of quartz vibrating at a constant frequency, stimulated by energy from a battery.

Experts believe that our bodies can act like a battery. We can stimulate crystals in such a way that they can have a beneficial effect on our well-being. It is said that if we place crystals close to us, our bodies will tune in to the vibrational frequency and be energised and healed.

If you have a gas oven, you may use a special lighter wand to create a spark. This tool has a piece of quartz built into it, which releases energy (the spark) when used, without any need of a battery.

One of the simplest ways to benefit from crystal power is to wear one or carry one in your bag or pocket, and at night take it to bed with you. It is believed that each stone emits a certain energy which is beneficial - but only if the wearer is receptive to its energies.

Thought patterns create energy. Positive thought is amplified by using a quartz crystal combined with our own natural healing power. This can bring much relief to many conditions.

It is said to be more a case of the stones finding us than us finding them, so if you feel attracted to a particular stone then you will benefit far more if you use that stone.

Once found, your stone should be cleansed before use. This can be done by simply cleaning it with cool water and then allowing it to dry naturally in the open air.

You can either hold it in your hand or at the side of you; relax, take a moment, and imagine your body, your mind and your crystal all in perfect harmony. This can be more beneficial if done last thing at night and first thing in the morning for a period of at least 10 days.

You will then be in a position to answer the question 'Is there hidden power in gemstones?' for yourself.

THE HEALING POWER OF CRYSTALS

N.B. The following information is not authoritative, but a fluid interpretation from many sources.

1. RED JASPER
A powerful healing stone. Can help those suffering from emotional problems by balancing physical and emotional need; its power to give strength and console such sufferers is well known.
Good for: liver, kidneys, bladder. Improves the sense of smell.

2. ROSE QUARTZ
Healing qualities for the mind. Gives help with migraine and headaches. Excites the imagination. Helps release pent-up emotions; lifts spirits and dispels negative thoughts. Eases both emotional and sexual imbalances. Increases fertility.
Good for: spleen, kidneys and circulatory system. Coupled with Hematite, works wonders on aches and pains throughout the body.

3. BLACK ONYX/AGATE
Can give a sense of courage, and helps to discover truth. Instils calm and serenity. Gives self control whilst aiding detachment.
Good for: bone marrow, relief of stress.

4. MOTHER OF PEARL
Aptly dubbed the 'sea of tranquillity'. Creates physical harmony of a gentle but persuasive kind. Calms the nerves. Indicates treasure, chastity, sensitivity and strength.
Good for: calcified joints, digestive system.

5. TIGER EYE
The 'confidence stone'. Inspires brave but sensible behaviour; fights hypochondria and psychosomatic diseases.
Good for: liver, kidneys, bladder. Invigorates and energises.

6. CARNELIAN
'The friendly one' - a very highly-evolved healer. A good balancer, can connect with your inner self. Brings good concentration, joy, sociability and warmth.
Good for: rheumatism, depression, neuralgia. Helps regularise the menstrual cycle.

CARNELIAN/AMETHYST

The Carnelian, when coupled with Amethyst, purifies the consciousness, reverses negative thoughts and develops higher mental awareness.

Good for: shaking off sluggishness and becoming vigorous and alert.

7. GREEN AVENTURINE

Stabilises through inspiring independence, well-being and health. Acts as a general tonic on the physical level. A stone to encourage a higher level of meditation. Favoured by Carl Fabergé, the Russian craftsman famous for Fabergé Eggs. A talisman, a bringer of good fortune.

Good for: skin conditions; losing anxiety and fears.

8. RHODONITE

Improves memory; reduces stress. Gives confidence and self-esteem. Cheers the depressed, preserves youth and retards the ageing process. Helps to bring back the life force into the sick. Carries the power to the unobstructed love. A very special stone.

Good for: emotional trauma, mental breakdown; spleen, kidneys, heart and blood.

9. SODALITE

Calms and clears the mind, enhancing insight and communication with the higher self. Brings joy and relieves a heavy heart. When placed at the side of the bed, it can make a sad person wake up full of the joys of spring. Imparts youth and freshness to its wearer.

Good for: When combined with Rhodonite, can produce the 'Elixir of Life'.

10. OBSIDIAN SNOWFLAKE

For all those it recognises, it is a powerful healer. Keeps energy well grounded, clears subconscious blocks and brings and insight and understanding of silence, detachment, wisdom and love. A lucky talisman, a bringer of good fortune. Favoured by ancient Mexican cultures to neutralise negative magic.

Good for: eyesight, stomach and intestines.

11. BLUE ONYX/AGATE

Improves the ego. A supercharger of energy; a stone of strength and courage. Aids concentration and helps to soothe all kinds of hostile feelings, allowing joy into your life. Inspires serenity.

Good for: stress; certain ear disorders.

12. AMETHYST

Aids creative thinking. Relieves insomnia when placed under pillow. A very special and powerful aid to spiritual awareness and healing. Very helpful for meditation, inspiration, intuition and divine love. When worn with Carnelian it will calm the overactive. A 'love and romance' stone.

Good for: blood pressure, fits, grief, insomnia.

13. HEMATITE

A stone you either like or dislike. To those who like it, it can be a very optimistic inspirer of courage and magnetism. Lifts gloominess and depression. When used in conjunction with Carnelian it can prevent fatigue. This stone is particularly effective during pregnancy.

Good for: blood, spleen; generally strengthens the body.

14. ROCK CRYSTAL

This stone holds a place of unique importance in the world of gems. It enlarges the aura of everything near to it and acts as a catalyst to increase the healing powers of other minerals. Its vibrations resonate with a triple-time, waltz-like beat of life, giving it a co-ordinating role in all holistic practices. It is the stone most favoured for crystal gazing. Good for: brain, soul; dispels negativity in your own energy field.

15. MOONSTONE

Gives inspiration and enhances the emotions. A good emotional balancer; a solid friend, inspiring wisdom. In India the Moonstone is a sacred gem, thought to be lucky if given by the groom to his bride. Good for: period pain and kindred disorders, fertility and childbearing.

A GUIDE TO THE POWER WITHIN
POWER GEMS

A unique group of Gemstones and Crystals, carefully linked in harmony to unite their individual mystic powers and provide a Holistic Force which can revive Health, increase Wealth, bring Peace and provide Energy.

The concept of being treated by a lump of rock may sound odd and hard to imagine, but ancient civilisations have been doing just that since the dawn of time. Traditions, myths and supernatural stories have always been associated with the magical mysteries of Crystals, Minerals and Gemstones. For thousands of years, people have told extraordinary stories about the power that has come from within these stones.

The Sumerians and Babylonians, then the Egyptians and the Greeks, and even our own English ancestors not only believed in these healing properties, but actually used crystals and gemstones for treating a wide range of ailments and conditions in everyday life.

These ancient beliefs may have been lost or rebuffed for the last few hundred years, but some of these legends have now been proven to be close to the truth. Remarkable stories of complete recoveries after years of pain and misery are now becoming commonplace.

If just one crystal or gemstone does possess such power and does have such a potency, then just imagine how exciting the prospect is, of having three crystals and gemstones linked together. The thought of such power from each stone, united with the powers of others and amplified, is awesome.

Most Power Gems contain three gemstones or crystals, a powerful number, being representative of Mother Earth as well as the Holy Trinity.

POWER GEM TITLES

HEALER
We have united the three most powerful healing Gemstones and Crystals.
CARNELIAN
The friendly one. It is a very highly evolved healer, mentioned many times in both the Old and New Testaments of the Bible.
RED JASPER
Well known as a powerful healing stone and a provider of strength. Mentioned in the New Testament in Revelations 21:19 – "The first foundations of the walls of the New Jerusalem were made of Jasper". Represents Aries in Astrology, the first energy of the life cycle – "On the first day of Spring, a commencement force of purest energy revitalises the Earth".

ROCK CRYSTAL

This stone holds a place of unique importance in the world of gems. It enlarges the aura of everything near to it and acts as a catalyst to increase the healing powers of other minerals. Co-ordinates all holistic practices.

Power Phrase :- Healing

GOOD LUCK

The three most powerful Gemstones, known for their good fortune.

OBSIDIAN SNOWFLAKE

Favoured by ancient Mexican cultures to neutralise negative magic. A very lucky talisman, a bringer of good fortune.

GREEN AVENTURINE

Green is a colour associated with God, and in Astrology is linked with Libra. Libra is the cardinal Air sign of the Zodiac and Air is the Breath of Life. Libra is also the seventh sign of the Zodiac, which is also favoured as God's number. Green Aventurine was favoured by Carl Fabergé, the Russian craftsman famous for "Fabergé Eggs".

MOONSTONE

In India, Moonstone is a sacred gemstone and is given to the bride by the groom on their wedding day, as a token of good luck and fortune. The moon has the most influence and power of all the heavenly bodies over our Earth.

Power Phrase :- My luck's returned, I give thanks.

ADULTS ONLY

These powerful stones combine to create the most imaginative aphrodisiac. A very sensuous combination.

ROSE QUARTZ

Well known as a love stone with a beautiful colour of pink.

AMETHYST

A romantic stone, very helpful for meditation, inspiration and divine love.

CARNELIAN

A stone used on the breastplate of King Solomon. This power stone represents passion and energy and, like Amethyst, Carnelian contains iron traces which give it its seductive colour. A solid, dependable stone.

Power Phrase :- Bring my lover to me

FOR WILLPOWER

The most powerful combination of stone and crystal which can be used to boost the willpower, e.g. to lose weight or stop smoking.

ROSE QUARTZ

Healing qualities for the mind, helps to release pent up emotions whilst dispelling negative thoughts.

BLACK ONYX

It can give a sense of courage and helps to discover truth. Gives self control, whilst aiding detachment. Helps relieve stress.

ROCK CRYSTAL

This stone holds a place of unique importance in the world of gems. It enlarges the aura of everything near to it and acts as a catalyst to increase the healing powers of other minerals. Co-ordinates all holistic practices.

Power Phrase :- I can and I will

TO REMOVE ACHES AND PAINS

Three Gemstones designed for easing aches and pains.

ROSE QUARTZ

Rose Quartz is made up of minute crystals with traces of Titanium, a metallic element, which give it profound strength.

HEMATITE

There are many ailments which benefit from a source of iron. When united with Rose Quartz, this steel-like stone works wonders with aching bones and bruised skin.

ROCK CRYSTAL

Once again the power of Rock Crystal acts as a catalyst to increase the active powers within Rose Quartz and Hematite.

Power Phrase :- Healing light, shine on me.

PEACE OF MIND

A combination of stones to bring peace, harmony and tranquillity into your surroundings, to capture stillness in movement.

GREEN AVENTURINE

Green is said to be God's colour. A stone well known for easing anxiety and fears. A talisman, a bringer of good fortune.

ROSE QUARTZ

A love stone, which also helps to relieve migraine and headaches. Releases pent up emotions and high spirits, and dispels negative thoughts.

RHODONITE

Improves memory, calms the mind, reduces stress, gives confidence and self-esteem. Cheers the depressed, preserves youth and retards the ageing process. A very special stone.

Power Phrase :- Relax

ENERGY BOOSTER

A combination of three Gemstones to boost energy.

CARNELIAN

Good for shaking off sluggishness and helping us to become more vigorous and alert. A Gemstone used on the breastplate of King Solomon, maybe to boost his energy, perhaps because, as we know, he had 1,000 wives. Carnelian is associated with Virgo, the sixth sign of the Zodiac, and the element Earth.

AMETHYST

When coupled with Carnelian, Amethyst becomes a very powerful energy booster. Amethyst is tinted by irradiated iron, and iron is one of the six active body minerals essential for life. It strengthens muscles, enriches the blood and increases resistance to illness.

ROCK CRYSTAL

Has the power to enlarge the aura of other Gemstones, and in this case it increases power to store energy. In Greek mythology, Rock Crystal was known as Holy Water, frozen by the gods of Olympus.

Power Phrase :- Energy, Vitality and Strength

TO LIFT DEPRESSION

Three Gemstones which bring joy and happiness, and remove sadness.

CARNELIAN

The friendly one. Carnelian is a highly evolved healing stone. Provides good concentration, and brings joy, sociability and warmth.

HEMATITE

To those who like it, it can be a very optimistic inspirer of courage and personal magnetism. Lifts gloominess and depression.

TIGER EYE

Inspires brave but sensible behaviour. The confidence stone, fights hypochondria and psychosomatic diseases.

Power Phrase :- From sorrow to joy

ELIXIR OF LIFE

To produce an Elixir of Life, we should first wash the Gemstones, then place them in a glass of clear water and leave them overnight, ideally in the light of a full moon. The Elixir of Life should be sipped slowly in a ritualistic manner. This is a powerful approach, which appeals directly to the imagination.

RHODONITE

Preserves youth and retards the ageing process. Helps to bring back the life force into the sick, carries the power to the unobstructed love. A very special stone.

SODALITE

Brings joy and relieves a heavy heart. Imparts youth and freshness to its wearer.

Power Phrase :- Life force, grow in me.

IMAGINE

I used the lovely title from John Lennon's song "Imagine", as these stones really are designed for a very special purpose. Power beyond imagination holds the key to all changes of life. The fine tints of these stones are designed to help us reach a level within the mind where all things become possible.

ROSE QUARTZ

Helps to excite the imagination; helps to relieve pent up emotion. Lifts spirits and dispels negative thoughts.

AMETHYST

Aids creative thinking. A very special and powerful aid to spiritual awareness. Very helpful for meditation, inspiration and intuition.

GREEN AVENTURINE

Green is said to be God's colour. Stabilises through inspiring independence. A stone to encourage a higher level of meditation.

Power Phrase :- Imagination

See your local stockist first, for any Gemstones and Crystals
mentioned in this publication

For further details – write to:
Rosewood
P.O. Box 219, Huddersfield, West Yorkshire, HD2 2YT
e-mail enquiries to: **info@rosewood-gifts.co.uk**
Or why not visit our website for even more information:

www.rosewood-gifts.co.uk

POWER GEMS

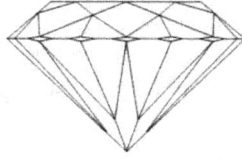

POWER BEYOND IMAGINATION

Many scholars and philosophers have stated that man is master of his own destiny.

Man has fully mastered his environment: planet earth, the land, the seas and the skies. He can travel around his world at will. He has built bridges and dug tunnels; he can travel both under and over water; he can fly higher and faster than any bird; he has travelled millions of miles in space, and has successfully been to the moon and back.

What makes man so special? He has learned to use the power of imagination, from deep inside the subconscious part of his mind, to conquer his environment and create the machinery to conquer the whole planet.

Having knowledge of the powers of your subconscious mind leads straight to the super-highway of the mind, which brings forth all kinds of riches, including spiritual, mental and physical, as well as financial.

Understand that energy, translated into thoughts, emotions and feelings, is the cause of all our experience, and so the cause of all effects.

With this powerful thought in mind, we should learn how to use this powerful subconscious power - a power that can heal the sick, lift fear and depression, and free us from the restrictions of poverty, want and misery. It can break the chains of repression for ever.

All we have to do is to be quite clear of the needs we wish to embody, and the creative powers of our subconscious mind will respond accordingly.

Draw deep upon the 'power beyond imagination', and you will uncover a completely new experience.

The Bible says, in a simple, clear and beautiful way: 'Whosoever shall say unto this mountain: be thou removed, and be thou cast into this sea; and shall not doubt in his heart, but shall believe that those things which he saith shall come to pass; he shall have whatsoever he saith.

Therefore I tell you, whatever you ask for in prayer, believe that you have received it, and it will be yours.'
MARK 11:23

In learning how to use our inner powers, we can open the prison doors of fear and enter into a life described by Paul as 'the glorious liberty of the sons of God'.

Discover the magic within the mind

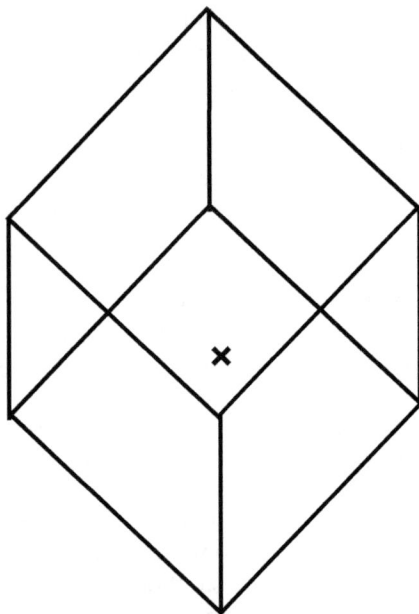

JUST LOOK AT THE CROSS FOR A WHILE AND SEE THE PICTURE CHANGE. YOU WILL THEN HAVE EXPERIENCED THE WORKING OF THE MAGIC WITHIN THE SUBCONSCIOUS MIND.

POWER GEMS
Three Magic Steps

STEP ONE

Find a peaceful and quiet place. Relax completely; empty your mind of the worries of the day. Relax into a sleepy, drowsy state, but try not to fall asleep. In this relaxed, peaceful, receptive state we are now ready for step two.

STEP TWO

Concentrate on a short phrase - a 'power phrase' - which you can easily remember and repeat over and over again, like a lullaby or Mantra. This can be done within the quiet of your mind, or, better still, spoken softly out loud. This will help it to enter your subconscious mind. Repeat this for five or more minutes, three or four times each day.

STEP THREE

As you are going to sleep each night, practise the following technique. Repeat your 'power phrase' - for example, 'Health' - quietly, easily and feelingly. Do this over and over again, just like a lullaby. Lull yourself to sleep with the word 'Health'. Within a short period, your life should start to be transformed. You will be amazed at the result. Your health should improve dramatically, thus proving you have control of the power of your subconscious mind.

To ensure the most effective enforcement of your affirmation, you should also repeat STEP THREE first thing in the morning as you awake, and touch your Power Gem lightly. Once you can instinctively touch your stones and repeat your 'power phrase' on waking, you have arrived at a level of mind that will bring about all the changes you desired.

The phrase 'Health' can be substituted by any one of the other power phrases. The appropriate Power Gem should be at your bedside at all times.

A Special

Glossary

of

Healing Stones

Plus Birthstones

By
Robert W Wood D.Hp
(Diploma in Hypnotherapy)

Rosewood Publishing

BK2

CRYSTAL HEALING

The source of Love, Protection, Health and Security which we all seek comes from a UNIVERSAL LIFE FORCE which we often call God. To receive such a gift and have it work for us, we have to value it by listening, and then responding with our willingness to receive it.

How do we receive? ... Through the mind.

If prayer is the asking, then meditation is the listening - and Mother Nature has produced some wonderful tools, in the form of Gemstones and Crystals, to help us to receive the answers to our constant requests for help.

How strange, though, that we have such wonderful minds that can so easily appreciate the natural beauty of earth's abundance on the one hand, and yet, on the other hand, this same mind seems - even when we don't want it to be - distracted, easily wandering off from one subject to another. How easily we seem to catch irrational fears and phobias ... How difficult for us to change, even though we want to. How fearful a new day can become ...

Why is it that, for no known reason, we get feelings of unease, distress and even confusion?

Why is it that things seem to go wrong?

One answer seems to be: 'It's simply the way we are.'
Luckily, life doesn't want things to go wrong, nor for us to be out of balance with Nature, and fortunately seems to have produced many ways to help restore our *natural, intended state of balance.*

However, there may be a paradox here, in that the very thing we search for, we may already have. That is: built in to the **life force** is the ability to *heal*, to *change*, and to *discover* for ourselves a state of mind often referred to as ... *Peace of Mind.*

The most precious Crystal of all is ... OURSELVES.

So why not TURN IT ON and TUNE IT IN?

Prayer ..... is the **Asking**

    Meditation ..... is the **Listening**

        Crystals ..... are the **Tools for the Job**

This booklet deals with the tools: *Gemstones & Crystals*.

Although it's impossible to know in advance, one thing you can be sure of when using crystals is - that change will come.

Crystals are like amplifiers and transformers of energy. The smallest thought can be immediately enlarged by a crystal.

Crystals are tools, so it's not so much the Crystal that will do the work, but more the person who holds it, who can channel the energy for Change ... *Healing **through** the Crystal*.

Through the centuries man has used Crystals to treat many ailments and conditions. Ancient and Medieval records show that Crystals have been used to bring about remarkable results.

A very easy demonstration of the power held within Crystals is to simply take two quartz crystals such as Rock Crystal or Rose Quartz, or even Amethyst, no bigger than a small coin, and rub them together in the dark - and you'll see them spectacularly light up.

The mind is even more exciting. Just look at the picture of the staircase on the next page for a while - and when it moves, you'll be astounded by the effect!

THE SHIFTING STAIRCASE

In searching for connections within the mind, you need go no further than this picture. You will know what I mean if you just stare at it for no more than 20 seconds.

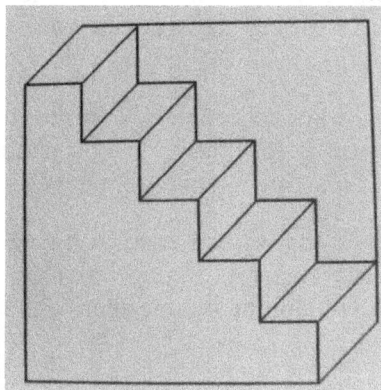

When you first look, you may see the staircase as if you were standing at the bottom right hand corner of the picture, ready to walk up the steps; then it will change, almost as if by magic, so that you are now in the bottom left hand corner, underneath the steps - or vice versa.

This change occurs in a fraction of a second, and it's this *change* that holds the key. **It's this *'change'* that, when connected to the stones, will bring about the desired *'life changing effects'*.**

*The **power** that created this effect is the **same power** that helps you to **connect**.*

Life is a journey - so enjoy the journey!

There are a number of other interesting pictures and a fuller explanation of how to use this natural effect with amazing results in my book, 'An Alternative View on Crystal Healing'. Here I am only dealing with the Glossary of Healing Stones.

The simplest way to use Crystals is for you to be connected to your chosen Gemstone or Crystal. This can be done in many ways, and all the different ways are intended to help you to connect mentally.

Effort of some kind has to be employed. If you bought a Crystal, brought it home, put it into a drawer and forgot about it, then the opportunity would have been missed and you would have wasted your money.

One of the simplest ways to connect is by holding the Crystal, or wearing it in the form of jewellery. Or you can use visualisation - hold the Crystal, and imagine a white light covering you and it.

Burying the Crystal in the ground enables it to be re-energised. To cleanse a Crystal, put it under a running water tap and allow it to dry naturally. The more you do, the more effective the outcome seems to be!

All these rituals ... and there are so many more; for example, you could produce an Elixir and take a sip every night just before going to bed, or first thing in the morning. You could wrap the stone in silk and leave it under your pillow. My mother has a piece of Amethyst under her pillow to help her sleep. I carry a piece of Green Aventurine in my money pocket, because it's said to be a money magnet.

In fact, your only limits are the limits of your own imagination!

In your search, may you find the Truth.

Glossary of Healing Stones

You may believe it's **God's Power**, or brought about by a **Universal Life Force**, or just simply derived from a natural state of **evolution**. I believe that the *Power to Heal* can be found within the mind, and more importantly in the **imagination**.

So the following list has been compiled using combinations of either two or three Gemstones-Crystals (rather than singles as often found in other publications), because combinations can have a very positive and powerful effect within our minds.

The following information **is not authoritative**, but is a fluid interpretation drawn from many sources.

PRECAUTIONARY WARNING: *It is always advisable to consult your own Doctor before embarking on any course of self-treatment or using any type of alternative therapy.*

NB: On no account should a Gemstone or Crystal ever be swallowed.

A

Aches & Pains (easing of) — Rose Quartz, Rock Crystal & Hematite
Abdominal Colic — Mother of Pearl & Obsidian Snowflake
Accidents (prevention of) — Yellow Carnelian & Tiger Eye
Addiction — Amethyst & Black Onyx
Adults Only (aphrodisiac) — Rose Quartz, Amethyst & Carnelian
Acidity — Green Jasper & Rock Crystal
Ageing (to retard general process of) — 'Elixir of Life' Sodalite & Rhodonite

Aggression (moderation of) — Carnelian & Amethyst
Alcoholism — Amethyst & Black Onyx
Allergies — Red Jasper, Rock Crystal & Carnelian
Anaemia — Citrine & Hematite
Anger — Carnelian & Amethyst
Angina — Rose Quartz & Amethyst
Animals (to cure illnesses) — Rose Quartz & Rock Crystal
Anorexia — Rhodochrosite & Rock Crystal

Anxiety	Rock crystal & Tiger Eye
Arthritis	Mother of Pearl & Carnelian
	Also Copper & Magnets
Asthma	Amber & Rose Quartz

B

Backache	Blue Agate & Hematite
Bad Temper	Blue Tiger Eye & Green Aventurine
Baldness	Aquamarine & Rock Crystal
Bladder	Jade & Red Jasper
Bleeding	Bloodstone & Carnelian
Blood Circulation	Sodalite & Carnelian
Blood Pressure (high)	Jade & Sodalite
Blood Pressure (low)	Sodalite & Carnelian
Brain Tonic	Amethyst & Carnelian
Breathlessness	Amber & Black Onyx
Bronchitis	Amber & Black Onyx
Bruises	Rose Quartz & Carnelian
Burns	Sodalite & Amethyst

C

Calming	Sodalite & Rock Crystal
Cancer	Red Jasper, Rock Crystal & Carnelian
Catarrh	Amber & Blue Agate
Cell Rejuvenation	Sodalite & Rhodonite
Central Nervous System	Rock Crystal & Rose Quartz
Chest Pains	Malachite & Rose Quartz
Circulation	Sodalite & Carnelian
Concentration	Carnelian & Red Jasper
Constipation	Red Jasper & Citrine
Coughs	Aquamarine & Blue Agate
Courage	Hematite & Tiger Eye
Cramp	Bloodstone & Amethyst
Creativity	Amethyst & Red Jasper
Crown Energy	Rock Crystal & Amethyst

D

Depression (to lift)	Tiger Eye, Carnelian &Hematite
Despair	Rhodonite & Carnelian

Diabetes	Rock Crystal & red Jasper
Digestion	Citrine & Obsidian Snowflake
Dreams	Rutilated Quartz & Jade
Drunkenness	Amethyst & Tiger Eye

E

Ear Problems	Amethyst & Blue Agate
Eczema	Amethyst & Green Aventurine
Elixir of Life	Rhodonite & Sodalite
Emotional Strength	Amethyst & Rose Quartz
Energy Booster	Amethyst, Rock Crystal & Carnelian
Epilepsy	Black Onyx & Tourmaline
Eyesight	Obsidian Snowflake & Rose Quartz

F

Fainting	Amethyst & Lapis Lazuli
Fatigue	Amethyst, Rock crystal & Carnelian
Fear	Rose Quartz & Rhodonite
Fertility	Rock Crystal, Rose Quartz & Moonstone
Fever	Carnelian & Red Jasper
Forgetfulness	Rhodonite & Unakite
Fractures	Mother of Pearl & Hematite
Frustration	Obsidian Clear & Rose Quartz

G

Gall Bladder	Red Jasper & Tiger Eye
General Tonic	Green Aventurine & Blue Agate
Good Luck	Moonstone, Green Aventurine & Obsidian Snowflake
Grief	Red Jasper & Obsidian Snowflake

H

Haemorrhoids	Mother of Pearl & Obsidian Clear
Hair	Aquamarine & Rock Crystal
Happiness	Carnelian & Sodalite
Hay Fever	Amber & Tiger Eye
Headache	Rose Quartz & Hematite
Hearing	Blue Agate & Rhodonite

Heart Disease	Rock Crystal, Red Jasper & Carnelian
Hypochondria	Tiger Eye & Blue Agate

I

Imagine (a key to Life)	Rose Quartz, green Aventurine & Amethyst
Immune System	Blue Agate & Carnelian
Impotence	Rhodonite & Sodalite
Indigestion	Jasper & Citrine
Insomnia	Amethyst & Sodalite
Intestine	Mother of Pearl & Obsidian Snowflake
Intuition	Amethyst & Rock Crystal
Irritated Throat	Amber & Rhodonite
Itching	Green Aventurine & Hematite

K

Kidney	Jade & Carnelian
Knees	Mother of Pearl & Blue Agate
Knowledge	Amethyst & Rock Crystal

L

Laryngitis	Amber & Rhodonite
Laziness	Hematite & Blue Agate
Liver	Rhodonite & Jasper
Loneliness	Rhodochrosite & Amethyst
Longevity	Sodalite & Rhodonite
Love (potion)	Rose Quartz & Amethyst
Lungs	Fluorite & Amber

M

Melancholy	Red Jasper & Carnelian
Memory	Rhodonite & Unakite
Menopause	Moonstone & Rose Quartz
Menstrual Cycle	Carnelian & Moonstone
Migraine	Rose Quartz & Obsidian Clear
Mouth	Sodalite & Tiger Eye
Multiple Sclerosis	Red Jasper, Rock Crystal & Carnelian
Muscles	Rock Crystal & Hematite

N

Nails — Rhodochrosite & Mother of Pearl
Neck (tension) — Hematite & Rose Quartz
Negative Energy (to dispel) — Lapis lazuli & Obsidian Snowflake
Nervousness — Rhodonite & Mother of Pearl
Neuralgia — Rose Quartz & Hematite
Nightmares — Amethyst & Rhodonite

O

Obesity — Black Onyx & Rock Crystal
Obsessions — Blue Agate & Black Onyx

P

Pain (to relieve) — Rose Quartz, rock Crystal & Hematite
Paralysis — Amethyst & Rock Crystal
Patience — Rock Crystal & Howlite
Peace of Mind — Green Aventurine, Rose Quartz & Rhodonite
Phobias — Obsidian Clear & Rose Quartz
Pregnancy (for strength) — Hematite & Carnelian
Prosperity — Green Aventurine & obsidian Snowflake
Protection — Tiger Eye & Obsidian Snowflake
Public Speaking — Amber & Tiger Eye

Q

Quarrelling (between couples) — Rose Quartz, Green Aventurine & Rhodonite

R

Red Blood Cells (to promote health) — Hematite & Amethyst

Rejuvenator — Sodalite & Rhodonite
Reproductive System — Rose Quartz & Moonstone
Rheumatism — Mother of Pearl & Carnelian
Also Copper & Magnets

S

Sadness	Sodalite & Red Jasper
Scar Tissue	Rose Quartz & Rock Crystal
Sciatica	Rose Quartz & Hematite
Serenity	Rock Crystal & Rhodonite
Sexual Appetite (to arouse & increase)	Rose Quartz, Amethyst & Carnelian
Shyness	Tiger Eye & Hematite
Sinus	Sodalite & Black Onyx
Skin Problems	Green Aventurine & Rose Quartz
Sleep	Amethyst & Howlite
Smell (to improve sense of)	Red Jasper & Tiger Eye
Sores	Green Aventurine & Amethyst
Speech	Rhodonite & Blue Agate
Stamina	Amethyst, rock crystal & Carnelian
Stomach	Mother of Pearl & Obsidian snowflake
Stress	Green Aventurine, Rose Quartz & Rhodonite

T

Teeth	Mother of Pearl & Calcite
Tension	Rose Quartz & Carnelian
Throat	Blue Agate & Amber
Thyroid	Rhodonite & Lapis Lazuli
Tiredness	Amethyst, Rose Quartz & Carnelian
Tumours	Amethyst & rose Quartz

U

Ulcers	Green Aventurine & Tiger Eye
Urinary System	Citrine & Jade

V

Varicose Veins	Aquamarine & Rhodonite
Vertigo	Red Jasper & Obsidian Clear
Vocal Cords	Rhodonite & Blue Agate

W

Wasting Disease	Red jasper, Rock Crystal & Carnelian
Weak Muscles	Amethyst, Rock Crystal & Hematite
Weakness *(general)*	Amethyst, Rock Crystal & Hematite
Will Power	Rose Quartz, Black Onyx & Rock Crystal
Wisdom	Amethyst & Carnelian
Wounds	Rose Quartz & rock Crystal

Live the Journey - the Journey is Life

If thinking is the rocket
Then believing is the propellant

If thinking is the birth of the desire
Then believing makes the connection to the
Power that makes it happen

Look at things not as they are, but as they can be.

You can accomplish almost anything if you believe you can. We all have God-given talents and abilities, if only we could learn how to use them.

Keep an open mind ... for many, Crystal Healing works and has proved to be very beneficial, so discover for yourself if you can be one of those people that can benefit.

See your local stockist for any Gemstones and Crystals mentioned in this publication.

However, if you are having difficulty in obtaining any of the stones mentioned, we do offer our own mail order service and would be more than pleased to supply any of the stones listed.

Most Gemstones and Crystals, with just a few exceptions - for example Mother of Pearl - can be supplied in the form of Tumblestones. These are smooth, rounded stones, ideal for use as a Birthstone or as Healing Crystals.

The nature of Mother of Pearl, and one or two others, prevents them being supplied as Tumblestones; however, we would be pleased to supply these in their natural forms.

For further details - write to:

ROSEWOOD,

P.O. Box 219, Huddersfield, West Yorkshire, HD2 2YT.

E-mail enquiries to: info@rosewood-gifts.co.uk

Or why not visit our website for even more information:

www.rosewood-gifts.co.uk

For your convenience, all the Gemstones and Crystals mentioned in this *Special Glossary of Healing Stones* are listed alphabetically below.

1	**Amber**		14	**Hematite**
2	**Amethyst**		15	**Howlite**
3	**Aquamarine**		16	**Jade**
4	**Black Onyx**		17	**Lapis Lazuli**
5	**Bloodstone**		18	**Magnets**
6	**Blue Agate**		19	**Malachite**
7	**Blue Tiger Eye**		20	**Moonstone**
8	**Carnelian**		21	**Mother of Pearl**
9	**Citrine**		22	**Obsidian Clear**
10	**Copper**		23	**Obsidian Snowflake**
11	**Fluorite**		24	**Red Jasper**
12	**Green Aventurine**		25	**Rhodochrosite**
13	**Green Jasper**		26	**Rhodonite**

27	Rock Crystal	31	Tiger Eye
28	Rose Quartz	32	Tourmaline
29	Rutilated Quartz	33	Unakite
30	Sodalite	34	Yellow Jasper

BIRTHSTONES

There are beliefs that Birthstones can have an influence or bearing on our lives. It is explained that our bodies reverberate to celestial vibrations, and that throughout our lives we have this 'vibration' of our ruling planets within our bodies. Never is this planetary influence so strong as at the time of our birth.

Using the appropriate Birthstone seems to contribute to putting us more closely in line with the energies of our astrological sign and its ruling planet.

It is believed that Birthstones were originally given to the new-born, maybe in the form of a pendant or a loose stone, so as to protect the child from harm and help attract and bring about good luck.

There are many Gemstones and Crystals associated with the Star Signs. After extensive research, this is my list.

ARIES The Ram   **Red Jasper**
21 March - 20 April

TAURUS The Bull   **Rose Quartz**
21 April - 21 May

GEMINI The Twins   **Black Onyx**
22 May - 21 June

CANCER The Crab   **Mother of Pearl**
22 June - 22 July

LEO The Lion
23 July - 23 August

Tiger Eye

VIRGO The Virgin
24 August - 22 September

Carnelian

LIBRA The Scales
23 September - 23 October

Green Aventurine

SCORPIO The Scorpion
24 October - 22 November

Rhodonite

SAGITTARIUS The Archer
23 November - 21 December

Sodalite

CAPRICORN The Goat
22 December - 20 January

Obsidian Snowflake

AQUARIUS The Water-Carrier
21 January - 19 February

Blue Agate

PISCES The Fish
20 February - 20 March

Amethyst

Next :-

Create a WISH KIT using a Candle, a Crystal
And the Imagination of
Your Mind

Create a
Wish Kit
using
A candle, a Crystal
And the Imagination
Of your
Mind

By
Robert W. Wood D.Hp
(Diploma in Hypnotherapy)

Rosewood Publishing

BK3

The key to happiness is having dreams.
The key to success is making dreams come true.

oOo

A wish

The feeling or expression of a desire or a hope for the future, either concerning your own or someone else's welfare, health, wealth, energy, luck, or piece of mind.

Wish fulfilment

The mechanism involving the release of tension, brought about by re-enacting in fantasy a situation in which a goal is attained.

A kit

A set of tools, supplies etc. for use together for a purpose.

A candle

Have you ever lit a candle for a prayer or to make a wish, be it in the privacy of your own home or in a church? It may have been just for decorative purposes, perhaps whilst having an evening meal, to create a romantic feeling. For whatever reason, have you ever noticed that within a few moments of the candle being lit, there seems to be a sense of calm, peace; a comfortable feeling being experienced? If you have, then you are already aware of the magic and wonder of candle-burning.

What is there about a simple flame that can exercise such a strong psychological, often almost magical effect on us? It's as if its bright light awakens an 'inner light' within us, and for that moment banishes the darkness of our deepest fears, our doubts and our worries.

The ancient saints, priests and magicians have all lit candles to help make wishes or prayers come true. Candles being lit for these purposes are the cornerstone of all the main religions.

oOo

A light will show you the way
And fill you with happiness

Crystals
Crystals and Gemstones have always been highly prized for their beauty, their ability to help attract good luck and fortune and their healing powers, as well as their mystical, spiritual like properties.

It seems that healers, shamans, priests and spiritual seekers have been attracted to these special powers since the dawning of time - powers that seem to inspire, delight, and capture the imagination.

The mind
The entity in an individual responsible for thought, feelings and speech, having the faculty of original or creative thought. Houses the subconscious: that part of the mind considered to be outside or only partly within one's conscious awareness, and the place where the imagination can be found.

The imagination
The faculty or action of producing mental images of what is not present or has not yet been experienced. Imagining something that is not immediately present to the senses often involves memory. Imagination is responsible for mental creative ability.

'Imagination is more important than knowledge' - *Albert Einstein*

An Analogy
Imagine you have just acquired the latest, the most stylish computer ever built. After unwrapping it, what is the first thing you have to do? **Plug it in**, of course.

So **it has to be connected to a power supply**. There must be a power supply; it has to be connected either directly to the mains or to batteries. **There are no exceptions.**

Then the next stage: it has to be **turned on.** If it's not turned on it won't work - agreed?

Then it has to be registered. You have to show you own it, often by providing a password, that's a code that only you and the computer know. This makes your computer different from someone else's; your password helps to make it personal and helps you to connect.

So you have plugged it in, turned it on and registered your password. So far so good; but it still doesn't do anything, does it? At least, not until you have connected it to a program. If that program is to connect you to the internet then **WOW**! Now you are connected to all the world's computers, you can email, you have access to all the accumulated knowledge stored on what is sometimes called `the information super-highway'. You can 'surf the net'. And all this is connected through a telephone, via cables, transmitters, aerial dishes and even satellites out in space.

NOW YOU'RE IN BUSINESS!

See a connection ... ?
> **Plugged in ... the Candle**
> > **Turned on ... the Crystal**
> > > **The Password ... Imagination**
> > > **The Internet ... the Mind**

The Subconscious

There seems a gold mine within all of us from which we can extract everything we need in order to live life to the full. It's a miracle-working power that's found in the mind, but more importantly in the subconscious - maybe the last place most people would look. You don't need to acquire it; you already have it. Learn how to use it, understand it. Through the power of the subconscious mind you can attract all the wealth you'll ever need, and the freedom to be, to do, and to go as your heart desires. You can attract the ideal companion, as well as the right business associate or partners. Through it, you can even find the right buyer for your house. Though invisible, its power is real. Within your subconscious mind, and more importantly within the imagination, you will find the solution for every problem or worry, discover the cause for every effect.

To stand any chance of succeeding with our wishes or prayers, we have to have a method for understanding. It's the same as the relationship between a program and a computer. To help to understand what I mean, let's look at the relationship between hypnosis and the subconscious mind.

Hypnosis, as understood by many psychologists, might be described as a state of excessive suggestibility in which a person seems to temporarily relinquish all conscious control of their behaviour. It seems they accept without question suggestions which in the conscious world they would recognise as blatantly irrational. Examples of this can be seen in the totally irrational behaviour of subjects at hypnotist stage shows.

Did you know that if you suggest to a person under hypnosis that the ice cube you have just placed in their hand is actually a burning ember, the subconscious mind, believing this to be true, will in fact produce a blister?

It's not unlike the placebo effect: a patient is given what they think is medicine, but which in fact is not; yet, remarkably, some people are cured. Think about it ... it's based on a lie, and yet manages to have the desired effect! The mind is truly amazing. To give you, the reader, the chance to experience this power for yourselves, let's try an experiment, using a pendulum.

A Pendulum
In my book 'How to Activate the Hidden Power in Gemstones and Crystals', I use pictures. One such picture shows a young woman who can also look very old, a little like a witch. Another shows a staircase that moves as you look at it. The front cover of my book shows an obelisk: when you look straight at it you can see only hieroglyphics written along it, but if you tilt your head you can see a word. These effects can be quite disturbing if you are not aware of what is happening. But remember: in all cases the effect is being shown to you to help you understand the power you hold within your mind. This technique is a very powerful, effective way of exciting the imagination, which in my opinion holds the key. I will now show you how to use a pendulum to produce the same effect as the pictures.

o0o

'When imagination and willpower are in conflict,

imagination will always win.'

o0o

Get a weight and tie it onto the end of a piece of string, so as to be able to use it like a pendulum. I have found that a simple key, like a Yale key, works just as well. You may have a crystal pendulum; this is even better. Now get a piece of paper, say A4 size, and draw a circle on it using a small saucer. Next, around the circumference put four dots, as if you were marking out a clock at twelve, three, six and nine o'clock. Then connect the dots making a cross; the point where the lines cross is the centre of the circle, and it's going to be a target. Place the paper on a table, sit down, and make yourself comfortable.

Hold the pendulum over the centre of the target. Steady it, if you have to, by allowing the pendulum to touch base, then lifting it just a little so that it is able to swing freely under the influence only of gravity. If you are uncomfortable, place your elbows onto the table to help support your arms. Whatever you do, **DO NOT MOVE.** Now, using only the power of you mind, imagine the pendulum swinging from side to side - and it will do so. Or imagine it swinging back to front or swinging in a circular motion either clockwise or anticlockwise. If it's not going in the direction you want, then imagine it changing direction and it will. It may be slow at the beginning. But it will change, and you will get better at it with practice. Try it - I know you'll be astounded. Remember, I am only showing you this effect to help you understand the principles behind a wish kit.

A Letter
A useful analogy could be: Imagine you are going to send a letter. First you have to address it. You then have to put a stamp on it, and finally you have to post it. After that, you have to trust it will be delivered. Consider the effort that has to go into sending it, say, to the other side of town, and compare that with the effort required to send it half-way round the world - but for you, you only need to post it, so don't worry about the HOW, just know it happens.

Wishful thinking
Don't confuse all this with wishful thinking. Wishing with the aid of a wish kit is more controlled and more precise. There is a method. In the church they call it prayer.

The power of prayer, if you have never experienced it, can be awesome, but it's not exclusive to a church, although it can certainly be found there. If you change the expression 'prayer power' to 'the power of thought', you start to get the idea of just what could be involved in delivering your wishes, as in the case of the letter.

As with the analogy of the letter, we all know that sometimes it seems to take ages for a letter or postcard to arrive. Some take a relatively short time, whilst others can take weeks. It may take a while for your wish to come true, depending on the wish or prayer. Within 30 days could be described as average. Some suggest the timing is linked to the cycle of the moon. You may object it could take 30 days for your wish to come to fruition.

I remember one wish or prayer took 18 months. However, it was well worth the wait when it did finally arrive.

Part of the method you'll read about is 'visualisation'. A key element of this is, **be very precise**. To give you an idea, I will tell you a true story and you can judge for yourselves whether the wish was, in this case, fulfilled.

A Sports Car

I was told about a man who tried out a visualisation technique: he physically went along to a Mercedes garage and collected many brochures on their 350 sports car range. He sat in the car to see how it would feel. He could smell the newness of the leather. He then found the best picture he could, in a metallic blue, and proceeded to cut it out, then went to his car and stuck the picture behind the sun visor. Every time he got into the car he would deliberately touch the picture lovingly and imagine the smell of the leather, until this just became a habit. Although after a while the energy had gone out of it, he still did the action of touching the picture every time he got into his car. Now here's the twist: a very good friend of his went out and bought the very same car, same model, same colour. His friend had never mentioned he was interested in this type of car. When the man went out with his friend, he found himself in the car, the very same one he had been imagining, even down to the smell of the leather ... well, was his dream, his wish, answered? Not quite - so be precise!

The Modus Operandi of Wishes

Start by mentally slowing down: take a deep breath, relax, and just let go.

Take a white sheet of paper (A4 will do), or a clean white hanky, and place it on a table in front of you. After a moment, when you feel quite relaxed, place a candle onto a saucer or small plate (to protect your table from the heat), Then place the saucer on your paper or cloth and light it. Use the suggested colour of candle, depending on your wish (see page 49). If you haven't got a coloured candle then use a white one; a simple, inexpensive nightlight will do. Now you are **plugged in**.

Now, having chosen the appropriate Crystal or Gemstone (refer to page 52), take it and place it gently between you and the candle. You are now **turned on**.

Next, take the appropriate colour of paper (postcard size is ideal) and write out your wish or prayer - this is to be done between you and the Crystal (see example of wishes on page 13). This represents your **password**; you are making it personal.

Then take the Crystal or Gemstone and wrap it up carefully. Turn it in to a little parcel. Write a word or two on it to describe your wish, for example: Love, Health, Friendship, Wealth, Luck, Peace, or just A Wish. Now place it by a window, to allow it to 'see out'. This represents **the internet**.

Then say a prayer of thanks, such as: 'Divine Mother, Father, Higher Self, Guides and Angels, thank you for granting my wish,' or 'For the good and love of all, thank you for ...' Remember to say it as if you have already received your wish. Not 'I hope' or 'if'; say '**I have**', in the past tense.

Now visualise the wish granted. See its fulfilment in your mind's eye, and then imagine how you will feel when it comes about.

Energise it.
Finally, blow out the candle, and wait a moment. You have just sent a kind of spiritual e-mail. Leave your wish in the parcel for up to 30 days and then you can retrieve the crystal, cleanse it, and it can be used again. Save the paper as a record of you wishes. Why not make a special box? It all helps to excite the imagination; and with the help of your imagination, you can move mountains.

Colour
Colour is important as a source of power. You may think it is stating the obvious to say that colour must be one of the greatest pleasures of life, although we probably all take it for granted. See the wonder of a sunset or the breaking of a new dawn, the splendour of clear night sky with a full moon, and the brilliance of the millions of stars. These things bring excitement to our senses and refreshment to our spirits. That's why it helps to boost the power of our wishes by using coloured paper for our wish or prayer.

**When powered by the energy of strong intention,
universal law becomes activated.**

There is currently no explanation that sits easily within the parameters of conventional science to explain how these things seem to work. There again, science can't explain the placebo effect despite accepting and recognising that it exists.

To help make your wishes come true, this exclusive 'Rosewood Wish Kit' draws from an ancient knowledge that's almost magical like, and yet seems so desperately needed in today's modern world. The following pages are divided into seven categories. Below, the appropriate colour of paper is given for each category. White can be used as an alternative for all the groups.

Category	Colour of paper	Colour of candle
Love	Red	Red
Health	Orange	Orange
Friendship	Yellow	Yellow
Wealth	Green	Green
Luck	Blue	Blue
Peace	White	White
Any Wish	Lilac	Lilac

The following are just some ideas on how to formulate a wish. You could write out, for example: *In the name of Love, I thank you for granting my Wish for.....*

LOVE	*finding my new partner*
HEALTH	*curing my illness.*
FRIENDSHIP	*sending a special friend*
WEALTH	*winning the lottery.*
LUCK	*finding my lost... ....*
PEACE	*giving me understanding*
ANY WISH	*the child soon to be born*

Ask most people about their goals - what they would like to be in, say, five years' time; how much money they want to have, what they want to be doing at work, at home or at play - and most will say they don't know. The truth is that most people don't. This is one of the most common responses and also one of the major reasons why people seem to fail.

In the Bible - Mark 11:24 - it is written: 'Believe that you **HAVE** received it', and not 'Believe that you **WILL** receive it'.

According to this piece of the Scriptures, we can receive a thing by believing we already have it, that it's already ours. This is why we make our affirmations, our prayers, our wishes in the present tense.

The following ideas are to help you focus on, and formulate, your own specific wish or prayer.

Ideas for Goals
To increase net worth (exact amount of invested capital)
To be self-determined, and allow others the same right
To increase income (exact amount should be stated)
To gain maximum energy easily, for use at will
To have warm and loving human relationships
To relax fully at will and avoid tensions
To increase overall self-concept
To stop all destructive criticism
To be responsible for yourself
To achieve a happy marriage

Remember, the best way to formulate a wish, or prayer, is to write it down so that when you read it back it makes sense and is affirmative, in the **past tense**. For example, if you wanted to attract a new partner, as mentioned in the 'love' section, then this is how you could go about doing it.

Find a piece of red paper and write on it your wish or prayer, in this case: *In the name of love, thank you for granting my wish and bringing me my new partner.*

Fold the paper around any of the crystals mentioned for love: Rose Quarts, Amethyst or Carnelian. Turn it into a little parcel; then write on it 'LOVE', and place it in the window.

Then come back to your lit candle and say a prayer of thanks, for example: 'Divine Mother, Father, Higher Self, Guides and Angels, thank you for granting me my wish (or Prayer).' Or: 'God the Father, in the name of your Son our Lord Jesus Christ, thank you for granting me my prayer (or wish).'

Find the way that is comfortable for you. If it feels right, then it probably is right. Trust your instincts - they have been developed over many thousands of years.

Next, imagine how you would feel if the wish or prayer you have just made is granted.

Feel it ... imagine it ... energise it ... and then let go. Take a moment, then blow out the candle. You have now disconnected yourself from a very powerful mental exercise - a little like when you disconnect your computer from the internet.

In church, it would be called a prayer. It really doesn't seem to matter whether you are religious or not; the facts seem to be that when help or assistance is required, then a universal life force, often called God, will help us to succeed, wherever possible - you only have to ask.

o0o

**'For everyone who asks, receives; he who seeks, finds;
and to him who knocks, the door will be opened.'**
Matthew 7:7-8

Some further ideas that may help to create or formulate your wish or prayer:

For ...Love
To keep a true love
To charm the partner of your dreams
To mend a broken friendship
To attract a new partner
To create a happy relationship
To arouse sexual passions
To find a soul mate
To put life back into a relationship

For ...Health
To stop headaches and migraines
To improve memory and concentration
To cure an illness
To gain greater vitality
To remove aches and pains
To overcome anxiety
To avoid panic attacks
To become pregnant

For ...Friendship
>To increase your circle of friends
>To attract a true friend
>To know you're loved
>To share love with someone else
>To find strength to support a friend at a time of crisis
>To find a way to comfort a friend who is suffering
>To forgive and be forgiven
>To mend a broken friendship

For ...Wealth
>To acquire money and wealth
>To win contests, lotteries and at cards
>To change luck for the better
>To attract a new business or offer of work
>To become self-employed
>To get back into work
>To attract golden opportunities
>To be promoted

For ...Luck
>To find a new home
>To succeed in business
>To always attract good fortune
>To always be on the winning side
>To be in the right place at the right time
>To be lucky in love
>To find the right partner, both in business and in love
>To always arrive safely

For...Peace
>To acquire peace of mind
>To always be in control
>To gain freedom from any doubt
>To gain self-confidence
>To keep a home in balance
>To change sorrow to joy
>To always travel safely
>To have a faith

For ...Any Wish
>To start a family
>To avoid trouble
>To gain new insights
>To forget the past
>To end loneliness
>To have the wisdom to make the right decisions
>To improve a poor business
>To overcome depression

o0o

**If you knew you could have anything you imagined
What would you imagine?**

o0o

To help choose your special crystal, the one that can help your wish, a list taken from my various books is provided below.

For Love ... Rose Quartz, Amethyst or Carnelian.

For Health ... Carnelian, Red Jasper or Rock Crystal.

For Friendship ... Moonstone, Carnelian or Amethyst.

For Wealth ... Green Aventurine, Hematite or Tiger Eye.

For Luck ... Obsidian snowflake, Green Aventurine or Moonstone.

For Peace ... Green Aventurine, Rose Quartz or Rhodonite.

Just a few Crystals and Gemstones with some further suggestions that may help in providing a focal point for wishes:

Jasper: A powerful healing stone with renowned mystical powers. In astrology, represents Aries, the first energy of the cycle of life.

Rose Quartz: Renowned for working wonders on aches and pains. A healer and a love stone.

Black Onyx: For willpower, helps with losing weight or giving up smoking. Instils calm and serenity, diminishes depression.

54

Mother of Pearl: Aptly dubbed 'the sea of tranquillity', calms the nerves and creates physical harmony.

Tiger Eye: Forget your worries with this stress-busting stone. A confidence stone, fights hypochondria.

Carnelian: Adults only, a stone for nights of love and passion. A friendly one, a highly evolved healer.

Green Aventurine: Well known as a money magnet. Acts as a general tonic on a physical level.

Rhodonite: Improves your memory and helps revive youthful yearnings. Calms the nerves and reduces stress.

Sodalite: Brings back the joys of spring, helps impart youth and freshness. Calms and clears the mind.

Obsidian Snowflake: A lucky talisman, and a bringer of good luck and fortune. Favoured by ancient Mexican cultures to neutralise negative magic.

Blue Agate: A super charger that gives energy and vitality. Improves the ego. A stone of strength and courage.

Amethyst: A love stone. Attracts love, helps to find that special partner. A romantic stone, also aids creative thinking and relieves insomnia.

Hematite: An optimistic inspirer of courage, magnetism and strength. Lifts gloominess and depression.

Rock Crystal: Increases the healing power, whilst boosting your energy field. Holds a place of unique importance in the world of Gems. Increases the powers of other minerals.

Moonstone: A fertility stone for extra help when starting a family. A good emotional balancer and solid friend, inspiring wisdom; a very lucky, sacred Gem.

Jesus said,

Everything is possible for him who believes.

Mark 9:23

oOo

Remember, a wish kit needs its tools just as Clark Kent needed a costume to complete his transformation into Superman. Our wish kit needs as its costume a candle, a crystal and the imagination of the mind. There is a simple truth about ourselves and the world we live in, and it is simply to *believe*. Keep an open mind. Belief pulls back the blinds of illusion and allows us to see the truth. This then carves a direct pathway into our inner world, where all our needs can be found.

Remember this, the power is within you and your belief...

oOo

See your local stockist for any Gemstones and Crystals mentioned in this publication.

However, if you are having difficulty in obtaining any of the stones mentioned, we do offer our own mail order service and would be more than pleased to supply any of the stones listed.

For further details - write to:
ROSEWOOD
P.O. Box 219, Huddersfield, West Yorkshire. HD2 2YT

E-mail enquiries to: info@rosewood-gifts.co.uk

Or why not visit our website for even more information:

www.rosewood-gifts.co.uk

Gemstone and Crystal

Elixirs

Potions for
Love, Health,
Wealth
Energy and Success

By
Robert W Wood D.Hp
(Diploma in Hypnotherapy)

Rosewood Publishing

BK4

Gemstones & Crystal Elixirs

Let your imagination fly you, on the wings of Love,
Into an ancient world of Magic, Mystery & Imagination.
By changing the way we think,
we can change the future.

o0o

"Elixir of Life":
An alchemical preparation
capable of prolonging life;
A liquid containing a medicine.

o0o

A Power Within

From the dawning of time, and hidden deep inside the subconscious mind within each and every one of us, there lies an amazing, invisible, gentle giant. One that can be stirred when touched by stories of Myths, Magic and Mysteries

Think of the popularity of the Harry Potter films, or Lord of the Rings. Who hasn't heard of King Arthur and the Round Table, or Merlin the magician? We like stories, especially mysteries; they feed our imaginations.

Now, in this book we're not describing a magic like that of magicians pulling rabbits out of hats.

We're talking of an ancient form of 'magic', the art of using lotions, potions, gemstones and crystals to awaken this giant within, to invoke the supernatural powers that we will need to help us change and influence future events.

Understand: we're not talking about witches riding on broomsticks or cooking up 'eye of newt' and 'toe of rat' in a bubbling cauldron. Instead, imagine a biochemist working in the very latest, air-conditioned, 'state-of-the-art' laboratory.

Today, science and technology are laying bare the secrets of the Universe; and one such secret that science has been investigating is the workings of the mind, both the conscious and the subconscious. However, our understanding of the power that's within the mind is still in its infancy. It seems that we are only now discovering just how amazing this 'power within' really is.

To discover this power that we are calling a gentle giant, let's try a little experiment. For example:- When you read the word 'witches and broomsticks', I'll almost guarantee you imagined an old woman in black. And when you read 'imagine a biochemist', you probably imagined him or her in a white coat. Most people do; we're programmed, and this effect that we call the 'imagination' was created by - well, if you believe in Darwin's theory you will say by evolution, or you may say by a universal life force that many today would call God. The fact is, we all possess this power, the power of imagination. We are the living proof.

**Henry Ford couldn't have built motor cars
before he had *imagined* he could.**

A Dawning of an Age
If the Piscean age was the age of Jesus Christ the man, then could the Aquarian age be the age when the spiritual nature of the Christ can be fulfilled and realised in all of us. Perhaps this is what is meant by the term 'the second coming'.

Moving from a great age of Christian religion, as well as religions from Asia and the Orient, the coming age is one of humanity; one that is not separated by religions, beliefs, creeds or dogmas. Emerging is a Golden Age, characterised by people living as individuals with their own beliefs about the world - but living in harmony, without any personal judgement of others.

A Freedom to Choose
One of the greatest questions must be, can we change our fate? Can we indeed affect the future? Or does it all just depend on the spin of a coin? The answer, I believe, is: yes, we can, at least to the extent that we have free will - that is, we have a freedom to choose. How

do we get help to change our future for the better? One way you are about to discover is with the help of Gemstone and Crystal Elixirs

Do Elixirs Really Work
I believe they do. To understand the 'how' and 'why', we need to look deeper into the three ingredients needed to produce a Gemstone and Crystal Elixir. Firstly there's water, and secondly, gemstone-crystals. But there's a third ingredient, often overlooked, but which I believe to be the most important ingredient of all: the Mind.

Firstly ... Water

Whoever is thirsty, let him come, and whoever wishes, let him take the free gift of the 'Water of Life'.
Rev 22.17-18

Imagine the flow of life being symbolised by water. It seeps into the areas of life that are inaccessible to other elements, which is one reason why it is associated with the subconscious, emotional and imaginative forces within the mind. Water is a unique substance, with amazing properties - either as a liquid, or a gas (in the form of steam), or even a solid (in the form of ice). Some describe it as a living substance, maybe with an energy of its own. It's even been suggested that water somehow has a memory, a structure that stores information, maybe in the same way genetic data is stored in the DNA.

Homeopathy
In homeopathy, for example, plant and animal extracts are dissolved into a solution. Most of the flower essences are prepared by floating the blooms in pure water for a number of hours. This is often called 'the sun method'. Others are prepared by boiling for an hour or so, this being more effective for the harder types of flowers and woody plants.

Mother Tincture
The mixture is then strained, and the resulting solution is known as the 'mother tincture'. Added to this solution is full strength 30-40% proof brandy, to act as a preservative. The 'mother tincture' is then diluted again, and again, and again;

in fact, by the time the remedy reaches its final stage, it is unlikely that any of the original substance remains in the solution, and yet it still seems to remain effective. However, the lack of evidence that there is anything there other than just pure liquid, may explain why some sceptics find it difficult to accept the efficacy of homeopathy. Supporters, on the other hand, believe that the science of physics is not yet developed enough to explain the phenomenon.

Secondly ... Gemstones and Crystals

It has taken over 4,000 years to prove scientifically what ancient wisdom teaches: that there is a force in nature so powerful, and yet to most of us quite invisible.

> **Now faith is being sure of what we hope for**
> **and certain of what we do not see.**
> **This is what the ancients were commended for.**
>
> **By faith we understand that the Universe was**
> **formed by God's command, so that what is**
> **seen was not made out of what was visible.**
> **Hebrews 11.1- 4**

It has taken quantum physics to show that solid matter is actually 99.9% empty space yet filled with energy. Now that we know that all matter is energy, looking at it this way may make it easier to understand how man can interact with gemstones and crystals.

Vibrations

Consider a tuning fork. When it is struck, and placed, vibrating, near the strings of a guitar or harp, only the string tuned to the same note or frequency will pick up the vibration and resonate. The rest of the strings will not; they remain unaffected.

The key to understanding the teachings of ancient wisdom may lie in the connection between the vibrations sent out by the perfect inner structure of crystals, and the human mind.

Crystals, unlike nature, have not evolved. It's said that they are the building blocks of the universe.

They haven't changed; they are exactly the same today as they were billions of years ago. Some even suggest they can be likened to the 'control experiment' used by scientists to verify the results of a parallel experiment. The variable which is being investigated in the parallel experiment remains constant in the 'control'.

Bound by myths, magic and mysteries, crystals seem to help bring to light the many different historical world views that have arisen down the ages concerning this immutable link between ourselves and nature. However, the spiritual connection between humans and inanimate objects such as crystals is not confined to New Age or pagan beliefs. In the Bible, stones and rocks were a symbol of human spirit and a representation of the higher self. Christ is referred to as a `living rock'

Gemstones and Crystals in the Bible
Gemstones and crystals are part of Creation. They have been written about for thousands of years, with some of the earliest writings being in the Scriptures. There's a piece in the Old Testament (Genesis) where God describes to Aaron, 'the first High Priest', how to produce a Breastplate, placing on it twelve gemstones and crystals. These twelve stones would represent the twelve tribes of Israel. Symbolically, there are twelve stones in Astrology to represent the cycle of life, and these are called birthstones.

Curiously, there is another list of twelve stones in the New Testament, here representing 'a New Jerusalem'. Even stranger for me was the discovery that the first foundation for the New Jerusalem was Jasper. Strange, because in my research I had already selected the same stone for Aries, which in Astrology is the first sign. The sixth foundation of the New Jerusalem was Carnelian, and I had selected this stone for Virgo, the sixth sign in Astrology; while the

twelfth foundation was Amethyst, which I had selected for Pisces, being the twelfth star sign. To discover how I got my selection of stones, you'll have to read my book 'Discover Why Crystal Healing Works', where I have given a fuller explanation of all the research I did.

Think of energy being channelled through crystals. However, crystals are only one form of tool, or catalyst, that helps to direct this inexplicable source of power, a power often referred to as the 'Universal Life Force'.

Elixirs

Whilst researching elixirs I often found conflicting information that only seemed to lead to more confusion, rather than clarify. So in an attempt to penetrate these mysteries, and especially Crystal Elixirs, I will focus only on elixirs and see if we can make some sense of it all. At the same time I believe we will discover a practical use for our newly gained knowledge.

A gemstone-crystal elixir is water into which a gemstone-crystal has been placed and left until the 'memory' of its health-giving or luck-changing vibrations is all that remains.

Warning

Some gemstone-crystals are unsuitable for producing elixirs, particular those that are soluble. Some gemstones and crystals should not be used under any circumstances as they contain poisonous toxins. However, all the gemstones and crystals mentioned in this book are quite safe. Do remember, though, to wash and clean them first.

It should go without saying that your choice of gemstones or crystals will depend on the results you want to achieve.

Gemstones and crystals have always been linked with Love, Health, Wealth, Prosperity, Energy and Success. Born from alchemy, a forerunner to our modern day chemistry, elixirs, lotions and potions were in times past only practised by a select few: priests, sages, holy men and magicians. Among these select few was Hildegard of Bingen. She was just one of the many famous recorded purveyors associated with gemstone elixirs.

Hildegard of Bingen

She was one of the outstanding females of the 12th century and probably of the entire Middle Ages. She was a painter, composer, poet, scientist, playwright, prophet, preacher, abbess – and a healer. Born in 1098, she lived until 1179, an impressive 81 years. From the time she was a young girl, Hildegard had experienced visions. Some of her ideas about Gemstones can be traced back to the Roman naturalist Pliny and other earlier authors such as Aristotle (4th century B.C.). Many of her directions or recipes involved the preparation of elixirs or the wearing of a stone, especially on the bare skin; soaking the stones in water or wine and then drinking the liquid or pouring it over the troubled spot. Hildegard claimed that angels described to her the healing properties of at least 25 stones. She describes putting an agate (stone) in water when the moon was full and leaving it there for three days and nights, then on the fourth day removing it and using the water for cooking the food for one who was suffering from a certain malady.

Feeling the need to share her visions with the world, at the age of 43 she decided to record what her visions had shown her. Hildegard consulted her confessor, who consulted the Abbot, who consulted the Archbishop of Mainz. Eventually, even the Pope was consulted, and all apparently agreed that these were true visions and her knowledge had come from angels, or at least some sacred source, and was worth recording.

Many of the earliest scholars believed that gemstones and crystals did have strange, often mysterious like powers.

Gemstones - Science or Myth?

If you take two quartz crystals and rub them together in the dark, you will see them light up quite spectacularly. Five thousand years ago, that would have been 'spooky' or even weird, certainly it would have been mind-blowing to anyone who didn't know the cause. Another example: if you put a lodestone near iron filings, the filings move, and people used to think this was magic. The stone, they thought, must possess mystical powers, or could even be alive.

However, today we know that this stone acts like a magnet, and the effect is quite natural.

Because of all the mysticism surrounding gemstones and crystals, it is not surprising to find that some scholars believed gemstones and crystals were alive. In Aristotle's writings we find descriptions of stones changing colour, especially when their owners were in danger from attack or poisons. Stones were even ground down to dust and then taken as we would today take aspirin for a headache.

I have spent many years researching and analysing as much information as possible, much of it spanning over many thousands of years. I have finally, from all of my research, produced my list of 15 basic (non-soluble) healing stones (pages 15-16), plus a range of Power Gems. These are combinations of stones relating directly to specific requirements; for example: Love Potion - Rose Quartz, Amethyst and Carnelian; for Good Luck - Green Aventurine, Obsidian Snowflake and Moonstone. See page 16 for many more.

In the next chapter we will explore the final ingredient that I believe is essential in producing elixirs, and that's the power within the mind. A power we call 'imagination'.

**To use your mind effectively
You must start by believing in its power.**

Imagination and the Mind

Although it's easy to see the importance of the first two ingredients - water and crystals - the third part, the mind, may well be the most important, and therefore could hold the key. The mind is often spoken of as unique and multi-faceted. That's an understatement. It's rather like saying the Universe is big: factually true, but it doesn't even start to scratch the surface.

The greatest philosophers of all time have pondered about the mind, the body, our emotions and feelings. The Scriptures say we are created and made in God's image. If that's true, then think about this:

There isn't, as yet (and I don't think there will ever be) a computer that could drive a car like a human being does. Think about it; how much information does a driver of a car take in during a normal journey? Doesn't that give you an idea of just how special we humans are?

Philosophy

Every existing being - from an atom to a galaxy - is rooted in the same universal, life-creating reality.

It reveals itself in the purposeful, ordered and meaningful processes of nature as well as in the deepest recesses of the mind and spirit.

My quest, and that of many others, is not to impose any dogma, but to point toward the source of unity that's beyond all our differences.

Many scholars have described life as being like a journey. The purpose may be to discover its meaning. What we seek outside, we may already own. Many others who have lived, loved and dreamed have left their legacies for the rest of us, in the form of their thoughts, writings, poetry and pictures, their beliefs and religions. They have all tried to explain the reason, the 'Mystery of Life'.

Power of the Mind

Let us accept that thoughts and emotions are all forms of mental energy, and that they play a very significant part in our well-being. It's believed we can influence the state of our physical body, either beneficially or otherwise, by the way we think.

Imagine this as an idea: Maybe it's the energy in thought that powers up crystals, just as electricity powers up a computer. Your own strength of will helps to direct, focus and amplify. Our natural state is one of moving towards balance, not away.

There is an important and potentially very happy marriage between the spiritual, the mystical and the scientific world views. So keep an open mind. There are many different methods of looking at the nature of 'reality'. This is only one of them.

Visualisation

You are now beginning to explore new dimensions of 'reality'. You don't need a spaceship, or to be spaced out, to take this journey. Just the will to find out more about yourself, and an open mind as you now take your own special journey into the future. The brain cannot tell the difference between what is real and what is realistically imagined.

That is why visualising is so powerful. Feeling, hearing, tasting, touching and smelling an imaginary experience is, as far as your brain's concerned, just as good as the 'reality', if the image had been real.

Have fun with your elixirs and your explorations. There is nothing unnatural about wishing to glimpse into the future or, for that matter, wishing to change it, particularly if you are given an opportunity to change it for the better.

Alchemy
Step back in time. Imagine yourself walking down one of the old Victorian shopping streets coming across a shop with a sign outside saying 'Alchemy'. You go inside - and, surprisingly, it's more like a modern day café. like the ones in York or Chester, and then you pick up the menu, and as you read it, you quickly realise it isn't food they're selling but magic potions and lotions, all guaranteed to work. Who wouldn't be tempted to try them?

You read titles such as `to Remove Aches and Pains', 'Energy Booster', 'to Lift Depression', and the speciality of the house, 'The Then you notice ...

The chef's special:
A Love Potion

Highly recommended: *Harmony*
For the more adventurous: *An Aphrodisiac*

Try them if you dare!

On page 72 is a list of the different elixirs and their formulas. So choose the one best suited to your desires.

Decide on the desired effect - are you seeking Love, Luck, Prosperity, Harmony, or something else? Next, choose the gemstone or crystal that in your opinion is best suited to your needs. You can use one, two or three of them, and you will find help on pages 71-72.

The Basics – Preparation

Start by purchasing two mineral water bottles, half-litre size with large screw tops. Empty one of the bottles and then place a label onto it, naming the elixir. For example it might be a Love Potion or maybe a Healer or even an Energy Booster. The choice is yours.

You may find the label puzzling, but it's really very important. Why? Because it acts on the mind, as an affirmation, and the mind works well with affirmations. There is a part of the brain that responds well to subliminal persuasion, so every time you use your elixirs, the act of reading the label reinforces within the mind your objectives, your desires. It reminds your brain what it is that you are asking for. So – make sure you read the label.

Once selected, take your gemstone-crystals and wash them thoroughly. Remember, these stones have come from all four corners of the earth. To be sure, I sterilise mine by boiling them for at least a minute. Once cleaned, then you can dedicate your crystal by saying something like:

**"I dedicate this crystal to love and will only use it
for the Universal benefit for all."**

In esoteric terms, this forms part of a spiritual ritual.

Then place the stones-crystals into the first bottle full of water, and screw the top back on. Now place a label on this bottle (sticky address labels are ideal) just saying 'Elixir'. Now place the bottle onto a window sill for three days and three nights, following the way Hildegard seems to have been instructed.

Note the time, and for the next two days or nights 'visit' the bottle at the same time, and touch it. While you do so, imagine your desired effects, but especially imagine how you will feel when they are achieved. Start building up the anticipation.

On the third day or night take the bottle from the window and shake it, to add energy, and pour the water into the other bottle. You now have your Elixir. Take the stones, dry them and place them into a safe place ready for the next time.

Some people like to put them into a silk purse, whilst others will plant them in the earth to re-energise. Others again lay the stones onto much larger pieces of rock crystal or amethyst. Do which ever feels comfortable for you. There are no hard and fast rules that I've ever come across. It's whatever feels right to you.

How to use
We now have the elixir, and the best way I know of using it is as follows. Take the bottle to bed with you, and just before you are about to go to sleep, take a small sip whilst at the same time using a visualisation to imagine the effect you desire to bring about. Add feeling and emotion to your thoughts by believing it's already happened. In other words, how will you feel when you do achieve your goals, your desires?

Therefore I tell you, whatever you ask for in prayer,
Believe that you have received it,
And it will be yours.

Mark 11-24.

Repeat these steps again first thing in the morning - and I do mean first thing, the very first thing, before even getting out of bed. You are trying to catch yourself still in the alpha state of mind. Once you can do this automatically, without thinking, you will have reached the level of mind where these things seem to work.

Place the bottle back in the fridge for storage during the day and bring it out again just before bedtime. Do this for seven consecutive days and nights, and Universal Life Force can't fail to get your message.

And finally ...
In hypnosis, if you give a person a glass of water and instruct them to "take a sip", then tell them they have just taken a truth serum and ask them a question, they will be compelled to tell you the truth, irrespective of the consequences. Be in no doubt. Imagine telling a person so shy that they have drunk a new drug that's just come onto the market and causes everyone who takes it to just ooze an amazing

confidence, becoming so attractive to the opposite sex that they attract admirers like a magnet. There's no doubt that this person will.

Or you could tell them they are so confident that they can't possibly fail their exams, or their driving test ...

The processes governing our subconscious mind, the power behind our imagination, our physical and emotional well-being, are all deeply rooted and nourished from the source of Life itself. The ability to contact this deeper source of life comes from within. So enjoy your journey of discovery. It's your journey

Although the following information is not authoritative,
it is a fluid interpretation from many sources.

Any information given in this book is not intended to be taken as a replacement for medical advice.
Any person with a condition requiring medical attention should consult a qualified doctor or therapist.
On no account should a gemstone or crystal ever be swallowed.

RED JASPER A powerful healing stone, can help those suffering from emotional problems. Its power to give strength and console such sufferers is well known. Good for: kidneys, bladder; improves the sense of smell.

ROSE QUARTZ Healing qualities for the mind. Gives help with migraine and headaches. Good for: spleen, kidneys and circulatory system. Coupled with Hematite, works wonders on aches and pains throughout the body.

BLACK ONYX It can give a sense of courage and helps to discover truth. Instils calm & serenity. Good for: bone marrow, relief of stress.

MOTHER OF PEARL Aptly dubbed the sea of tranquillity. Calms the nerves. Good for: calcified joints, digestive system.

TIGER EYE Inspires brave but sensible behaviour. The confidence stone. Good for: liver, kidneys, bladder. Invigorates and energises.

CARNELIAN A very highly-evolved healer. Good for: rheumatism, depression, neuralgia. Helps regularise the menstrual cycle.

GREEN AVENTURINE Stabilises through inspiring independence. Acts as a general tonic. Good for: skin conditions, losing anxiety and fears.

RHODONITE Improves the memory, reduces stress. Good for: emotional trauma, mental breakdown, spleen, kidneys, heart and blood

SODALITE Imparts youth and freshness. Calms and clears the mind. When combined with Rhodonite, can produce the Elixir of Life.

OBSIDIAN SNOWFLAKE A powerful healer. Brings insight and understanding, wisdom and love. Good for: eyesight, stomach and intestines.

BLUE AGATE Improves the ego. A stone of strength and courage; a supercharger of energy. Good for: stress, certain ear disorders.

AMETHYST Aids creative thinking. Relieves insomnia when placed under pillow. Good for: blood pressure, fits, grief and insomnia.

HEMATITE A very optimistic inspirer of courage and magnetism. Lifts gloominess. Good for: blood, spleen; generally strengthens the body.

ROCK CRYSTAL Enlarges the aura of everything near to it and acts as a catalyst to increase the healing powers of other minerals. Good for: brain, soul; dispels negativity in your own energy field.

MOONSTONE Gives inspiration and enhances the emotions. A good emotional balancer and solid friend, inspiring wisdom. Good for: period pain and kindred disorders , fertility and child-bearing.

oOo

You can use any of the gemstones or crystals mentioned here for your elixir. The following lists have all been taken from my various books; they may help you to decide. Also, to help, here are a few suggestions for that special elixir:

LOVE .... Rose Quartz, Amethyst & Carnelian

PEACE .... Green Aventurine, Rose Quartz & Rhodonite

GOOD LUCK....Moonstone, Green Aventurine &
                         Obsidian Snowflake
FERTILITY.... Rock Crystal, Rose Quartz & Moonstone

ENERGY........... Amethyst, Rock Crystal & Carnelian

HEALING .... Rock Crystal, Red Jasper & Carnelian

CONFIDENCE.. Tiger Eye, Green Aventurine & Black Onyx

PROSPERITY ... Green Aventurine & Obsidian Snowflake

ELIXIR of LIFE Rhodonite & Sodalite

FRIENDSHIP   Moonstone, Carnelian & Amethyst

See your local stockist for any Gemstones and Crystals mentioned in this publication.

However, if you are having difficulty in obtaining any of the stones mentioned, we do offer our own mail order service and would be more than pleased to supply any of the stones listed.

For further details - write to:

ROSEWOOD
P.O. Box 219, Huddersfield, West Yorkshire. HD2 2YT

E-mail enquiries to: info@rosewood-gifts.co.uk

www.rosewood-gifts.co.uk

72

Crystal

Pendulum for

Dowsing

An ancient Knowledge for Unlocking Psychic Power

By
Robert W. Wood D.Hp
(Diploma in Hypnotherapy)

Rosewood Publishing

BK5

CRYSTAL PENDULUM FOR DOWSING

**The purposes of a man's heart are
deep waters,
but a man of understanding
draws them out.
Proverbs 20 : 5**

Discovering a Miracle for Self-Help

Dowsing
Crystal pendulum dowsing is born from an art which in itself dates back many thousands of years. Mention dowsing to most people, and images of traditional diviners seem to come to mind - of men and women walking along through fields of green, holding with both hands a forked twig, one that looks a little like a wish-bone and seems to always be pointing upwards.

It's affectionately called a 'twitch', probably because it starts to 'twitch' just before it changes direction when it gets near to water, oil, minerals, gold or whatever the diviner may be looking for at the time.

Although hazel is probably the most popular material used, it seems to work just as well with ash, green elder or willow; even whalebone and common plastic have been used quite effectively.

Dowsing can also be done with other tools. A good example is a pair of metal rods bent into an `L' shape. It doesn't seem to matter what kind of metal the rods are; the dowser holds one in each hand, just as he would if they were a pair of guns, and when water - or any other substance he is dowsing for - is located, the rods move and cross over. This then marks the spot.

How does dowsing work?
There seem to be three schools of thought. One is that the dowser creates a bridge between the logical and the intuitive part of the mind, that is: the conscious (logical), and the subconscious (intuitive).

74

Another, that the dowser connects with a higher power, that is: that the information is coming from a 'divine' source, hence the name 'divining'.

Others say that it is electromagnetic energy, radiating from everything, that causes the effect. However, personally I fail to understand how a wooden or a plastic object can be influenced by an electromagnetic energy.

No one may know for certain, but I am going with the idea that there's a link with the conscious and subconscious mind. I think we will be on much safer ground.

Dowsing - a natural gift

In my opinion, the ability to dowse is a simple, natural gift of the human spirit, present in each one of us from birth. It's a simple method of bringing our rational consciousness safely into direct communication with our inner wisdom, our intuition, our subconscious. Although this may be difficult to understand at first, it will become clearer when you discover that the subconscious part of the mind is in some respects the most truly primary sense of all. It's certainly, you're about to discover, the most powerful.

Dowsing, then, is, when focused, a discipline that can help bridge the gap between the two levels of mind, the conscious and the subconscious, our inner and outer world. Our consciousness could be easily compared to the visible part of an iceberg, which everybody knows is only a tiny part of the whole. In fact, nine-tenths of an iceberg is below the surface.

Dowsing potentially gives us a means to have unlimited access to information, information which would normally be invisible and well out of view to the human eye, certainly well beyond the limitations of our five senses. Once you can dowse, you will find it possible to detect all sorts of things. It's like the difference between having a computer, and a computer that's connected to the internet.

Crystal Pendulums

New tools have been introduced over the years for dowsing, and especially, more recently, the crystal pendulum*. For the purpose of simple diagnosis for health, or gaining extra help for wealth, love, energy etc, the crystal pendulum is by far the most practical. It has the advantages of being very portable and easy to handle (much better than having to carry a large, forked stick in your pocket).

A priest's discovery

Whilst I was researching into dowsing, I came across this story, of a priest who, on his return from Ireland, had become very excited about his discovery of divining rods. Apparently whenever he prayed, the rods seemed to twist in his hands and cross over. He found this so exciting that he showed his parishioners, and in fact anybody else he thought might be interested. One of his parishioners, not feeling too comfortable about this, wrote to the Church and asked whether the Church encouraged or permitted this.

Now when push comes to shove, the shortest answer would probably be 'no', and indeed the answer did come back as 'no'. The reason given was that dowsing is a form of divination (the art or practice of discovering future events or unknown things as though by supernatural powers) and divination, as far as this Church was concerned, was occult and therefore must be forbidden.

So any practice that resembles it must be dealt with using extreme caution. The answer went on to explain that a prayer before or while using the divining rods might, in itself, render the practice innocuous; but it was still not recommended.

If one is trying to get supernatural information, then it is definitely, according to this explanation from the Church, of the occult. However, I don't think that's how the priest had seen it, nor do many others. You must judge for yourselves, but you are about to discover just how natural all this really is.

To help you experience what you are about to discover, I would like you to experience for yourselves this natural phenomenon. To help, read the following instructions and then try them out before you read any more. This will help you towards your discovery of a 'knowing'.

A Pendulum

In my book *Discover Why Crystal Healing Works*, I use pictures. One such picture shows a young woman who can also look very old, a little like a witch. Another shows a staircase that moves as you look at it.

The front cover of my book shows an obelisk; when you look straight at it you can see only hieroglyphics written along it, but if you tilt your head you can see a word. These effects can be quite disturbing if you are not aware of what is happening. But remember: in all cases, the effect is being shown to you to help you understand the power you hold within your mind. This technique is a very powerful, effective way of exciting the imagination, which in my opinion holds the key. I will now show you how to use a pendulum to produce the same effect as the pictures.

The following instructions are taken from my book Create a Wish Kit Using a Candle, a Crystal and the Imagination of Your Mind ('Wish Kit' for short).

Get a weight and tie it onto the end of a piece of string, so that you can use it like a pendulum. I have found that a simple key, like a Yale key, works just as well. You may have a crystal pendulum; this is even better. Now get a piece of paper, say A4 size, and draw a circle on it using a small saucer. Next, around the circumference put four dots, as if you were marking out a clock at twelve, three, six and nine o'clock. Then connect the dots, making a cross; the point where the lines cross is the centre of the circle, and it's going to be a target. Place the paper on a table, sit down, and make yourself comfortable.

Hold the pendulum over the centre of the target. Steady it, if you have to, by allowing the pendulum to touch base, then lifting it just a little so that it is able to swing freely under the influence only of gravity. If you are uncomfortable, place your elbows onto the table to help support your arms. Whatever you do, DO NOT MOVE. Now, using only the power of your mind, imagine the pendulum swinging back to front, or swinging in a circular motion, either clockwise or anticlockwise. If it's not going in the direction you want, then imagine it changing direction; and it will. It may be slow at the beginning. But it will change, and you will get better at it with practice. Try it - I know you'll be astounded. Remember, I am only showing you this effect to help you understand the principles behind this power within the mind.

A 'knowing'
Can you ride a bike? I know it may seem a daft question, and I bet you're wondering what it's got to do with crystal pendulums, but for a moment

humour me. So, can you ride a bike? I'll assume the answer to be 'yes'. Then - what was the difference from the moment you couldn't to the moment you could? It's a rhetorical question, because I think the answer is 'knowing'. Somehow, you seem to know you can.

It's like learning to drive a car: a little experience, some instruction, some effort, and hey-presto! you've passed the test. A few weeks later you're driving like everybody else. Something's kicked in, and I think it's a good example of this 'knowing'. Another example of this 'knowing' is: When you can drive a car, you consciously decide where you're going to go - 'I am going from here to there' - but you can't drive a car consciously. You need to drive it using your subconscious. You drive automatically - and you only have to see a learner driver learning to drive to understand what I mean. You can see them having to consciously 'think' about mirrors, brakes, clutch, gears, steering, signals, etc, etc. There's just too much information to be taken in consciously; however, when the subconscious takes over with this 'knowing', it takes everything in its stride and driving becomes very comfortable. It's strange, I don't think there will ever be a computer that can drive a car like a human being can. Therefore this 'knowing' is more powerful than any computer that has ever been built, or is likely to be. Other examples of 'knowing' could be swimming, typing, etc.

It's easier to learn how to drive a car than it is to learn how to build one. But just imagine if you did know how to build one; it would come in very useful if you ever broke down. My intention is, with this book, to give you a useful anchor, so if you ever do 'break down', you'll have the tools at hand to do a self-repair. I am going to guide you to a 'knowing'.

I've often heard it said that we shouldn't dabble in things we don't understand. However, by learning, and gaining knowledge, we can open the prison doors of ignorance and fear and enter into a life described by St Paul as 'the glorious liberty of the sons of God'. This freedom is gained when we have discovered our 'knowing'.

Beware of misconceptions

I recall an occasion when I was giving a talk to a ladies' luncheon group. My talk was entitled 'Discover the hidden powers of gemstones'*, and it had been well publicised. One of the ladies came up to me just before I was due to speak and told me she would have liked to have stayed and listened to me. However, she had apparently mentioned to one or two people at her church, in all innocence, how she was looking forward to hearing a speaker talk on what she thought would be a fascinating subject, but then was surprised to find that they seemed to object, and even went a stage further and suggested she didn't come.

On hearing this I explained that it was OK by me, and that my advice to her was that if it would make her feel uncomfortable in any way, then she should leave. Then she noticed I was wearing a Christian fish on my jacket. Although a little confused, she decided to stay, and so with some of her non-church friends she stayed and listened to me.

After my talk, she came over and told me how much she had really enjoyed it, especially the way I had linked Christianity and 'new age'. She then went on to say that she had made a decision regarding her own church. "I've decided," she said, "I am not going to tell them that I stayed." The fact that I had been talking in a kind of coded language about God's power didn't seem to have helped. It was apparently my use of the word 'hidden' that they had objected to.

What's in a word?

I discovered, years ago, that just one word on my posters was causing me no end of trouble, and once I changed it, the problem just vanished. The original line on my poster was: 'LEARN ABOUT BIRTHSTONES AND THE ORIGINS OF ASTROLOGY AS WE NOW KNOW IT'. Although it took me nearly two years to discover it, it was the word 'Astrology' that some, mainly within the church, objected to, so I changed the word and the line to: DISCOVER A CONNECTION BETWEEN BIRTHSTONES AND THE SCRIPTURES' and I haven't had any problems since.

* Now available on CD. Contact publisher or go online to www.rosewood-gifts.co.uk for further details.

Occult or Psychic?
Although the word 'occult' means 'hidden', not everything that's hidden is necessarily occult.

There is nothing concealed that will not be disclosed,
Or hidden that will not be made known.
　　　　　Luke 12:2

Psychic ... outside the possibilities defined by natural laws, as mental telepathy, sensitive to forces not recognised by natural laws, esoteric. Mental as opposed to physical.

Psychic speaks of apparent non-physical, yet human powers that emerge under certain circumstances and conditions. These could be primarily telepathy, clairvoyance and precognition (the ability to foresee future events). I believe we can include healing powers, and the faculties of dowsing as well. Another instance is the ability to see auras of colour or light around the human body.

Occult ... of or characteristic of mystical or supernatural phenomena or influences. Beyond ordinary human understanding, secret or hidden.

The word 'occult', on the other hand, suggests contact with spirit powers, black magic and witchcraft - all of which the author would seriously warn against. Most people will have heard of the 'Ouija Board'. It's a trademark for a board on which are marked the letters of the alphabet. Answers to questions are spelt out by a pointer and are supposedly formed by spirits. It isn't a coincidence that sometimes one of the questions asked at a preliminary interview before commencing psychotherapy is, whether the client has ever played with a Ouija board. I would place the Ouija board firmly into the occult category.

Natural psychic power
After reading the above descriptions, I hope you will agree with me that 'pendulum dowsing' falls safely into the realms of psychic power. I believe it to be natural and one of the most accurate ways of connecting back to

the inner self, whilst being at the same time the safest - safe because there's no third party involved to misinterpret.

We are using our own inner 'wisdom'. There is no break in the connection between the inner and outer worlds of the mind.

When asked about electricity, Thomas Edison is said to have replied: "I don't know what it is, but it's there, so let's use it."

Let's start by discovering our psychic power so we can help ourselves with our personal development, our dreams, our goals. Never forget that there is a power within, and that it can be summoned at any time and in any situation.

Just as radios receive information via unseen airwaves, so our minds act in the same way: our powerful antenna receives information from the vibrations and energy waves being continuously emitted by people, places, thoughts and things.

Throughout all the ages, man has striven in various ways to express his inner needs. The more simple and sincere he is in his wishes, hopes and prayers, the more successful he seems to be.

You can't get a much greater simplicity than the ability to dowse; it's a special natural gift of creation. For many, dowsing is a recognised method of bringing together the conscious mind (the 'gate keeper') and the subconscious (the 'inner child').

Some have described tapping into this 'inner world', the world of the subconscious, as like tapping into a rich vain of pure gold. Dowsing seems to be a way of bridging the conscious and subconscious parts of our minds whilst at the same time being able to sidestep the intellect.

Crystal dowsing therefore becomes an external expression of the internal. It's the visible bringing together of the mind and the spirit. Although dowsing may be thought of as an art or even a science, dowsing is really more 'holistic'; that is, a connection between the mind, body and spirit.

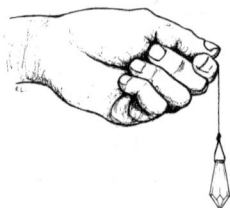

Illustration by Rachel Lubinski

Removing the intellect

The intellect is that part of the mind housed within the consciousness. It's the part of the mind that says, "This is all nonsense, this can't be, these things just don't happen." It's the adult speaking. It needs to respond intellectually, to always to give an explanation as to why.

This is one reason why the psychotherapist uses hypnosis to shut down this faculty. For psychotherapy to work, it's best if the intellect isn't there. Let me give you an example. A client says that they have an irrational fear or phobia of closed-in spaces, and they need help because they have just landed a position with a new company. Their office is on the fifteenth floor and because they're scared of closed-in spaces, they can't use the lift. They know they're being silly but they do need help. Then the intellect steps into the conversation and goes on and explain it's probably because their brother locked them in the broom cupboard when they were three.

However, let me say here and now that if a client ever says they know why they have irrational fears and phobias, but they are still having them, then the reason they give is not the original cause of their problems. There is a 'law of cause and effect' (trust me, I am a hypnotherapist!).

"I tell you the truth, anyone who will not receive the Kingdom of God like a little child will never enter it."   Luke 18 -17

Was psychotherapy around all those years ago? I wonder.

82

Having been asked when the Kingdom of God would come, Jesus replied, "The Kingdom of God does not come visibly, nor will people say 'Here it is' or 'There it is', because the Kingdom of God is within you." Luke 17 : 20-21.

Our subconscious mind can be likened to that of a child.

The basic principles
At its simplest, crystal dowsing involves asking questions to help seek out information not readily available by any other means.

You are about to discover that the uses for dowsing are only limited by our imagination.

When we ask our 'dowsing question', we are asking with our intellectual, rationally-thinking, conscious part of the mind. We ask a clear, unambiguous question in our mind. Then, having asked, we wait for the reply - a little like waiting for an internet search.

The answer, when it comes, comes in the form of movement. The crystal pendulum will begin to move either from side to side or from back to front, or even circling clockwise or anti-clockwise.

This is the external expression of our inner world - the inner world of the subconscious - where you'll find intuition, our sixth sense. From the previous experiment you will be quite familiar with the pendulum movements. Now we will learn how to interpret these movements, and it couldn't be easier.

It's not a panacea
Do you suffer from medical problems that won't respond to medical treatment? Do you feel that your luck's just run out? Can't find the right partner, however hard you look? Need to gain more energy, change your career, your life-style? Although you may not believe this, your problems could be being caused by repressed emotions, by incorrect subconscious thinking. The following may help to show if the true cause of your problems resides within your mind. Although crystal dowsing is not a panacea, you're about to discover how it can go a long way towards helping.

**Start here by tuning into your psychic energy
for your personal development and well-being.**

Instructions

Although it's not strictly necessary to sit or stand in a special way, a good posture often helps to relax.

Hold the cord of your pendulum between the thumb and forefinger, just as if you were holding a plate, in your dominant hand. (That is your right hand if you are right-handed, or left if left-handed). In my crystal healing demonstrations I always suggest that for best results the healing crystals should be held in the passive hand, so as to receive.

You will by now, after following the 'Wish Kit' instructions, realise that pendulums respond and move in regular patterns, either from left to right, or front to back, either circularly clockwise or anti-clockwise.

We are now ready to start our communications by asking some simple questions so as to learn the meaning of the responses. We need to ask questions for which there's a clear, unambiguous 'yes' or 'no' response.

When the pendulum becomes still and stops swinging, then ask a question to which you know the answer can only be 'yes'. Ask the question out loud or as a thought within your mind, both methods are equally effective.

Make the questions simple, for example: 'My name is ...,' and say your name; or 'Today's day is ...,' and name the day; or 'My shoes are ... ' and name the colour; you get the idea! Make a note of the direction, ask a few more 'yes' questions and confirm the pendulum still travels in the same direction. This then becomes your 'yes' response. Repeat it all again for a 'no' response. If you find you are getting inconsistent responses - stop, relax and start again.

Try some exercises

From this point you can play some games to exercise your new-found knowledge. Ideally, practice exercises in dowsing should be fun and engaging; after all, you are communicating with your inner wisdom, the subconscious, the part some call the 'inner child'.

For these exercises you're asking questions to which the answers can only be 'yes' or 'no'. Any ambiguity will only make the exercise very difficult to follow.

For example, start with a simple hiding game such as hiding a ball under a cup and dowsing to find its position. Playing cards can be a very good exercise. Take an ordinary pack of cards, take out the jokers, shuffle the pack and then lay them out face down. Using the pendulum, start by identifying whether the top card belongs to the black or red suits. Place your pendulum over the card and ask clearly in your mind, "Does this card belong to one of the black suits?" It's either a 'yes' or a 'no' response. Go through the whole pack, then see just how close you came. Remember, we are trying to establish a connection with a part of ourselves that will have been dormant for quite a long time, so we can afford to be patient and take the time to wake it up slowly and gently.

Once we are clear about our responses and familiar with the use of the pendulum, we can start to use dowsing on a regular basis in our everyday life.

Become your own psychic investigator
Whatever your problems seem to be, why not start by checking if you are the victim of unconscious, self-limiting, negative conditioning? Now you are becoming familiar with crystal dowsing as a technique for communicating with the subconscious, start by asking questions. For example: "Is my (name the problem or symptoms) due to an event from my past that still troubles me or upsets me in any way?" "Is my (name the problem or symptoms) due to an event from my past that has conditioned me to respond in this way?" I would ask the question a few times to check the response, and change the way the question is formulated.

Remember: you should always consult your medical practitioner or advisor. Crystal dowsing should not become the only method of diagnosing your problems.

To help you, here's a little more information as we delve deeper into the mind. The more you know, the greater your freedom. Here's more of a 'knowing'.

Brain waves

For all the advances of modern society, we cannot afford to ignore the ancient rhythms of the brain within all of us, any more than we could neglect our need to eat or sleep. Our state of mind is important for our dowsing to be effective, and the most powerful states of mind for our purposes here are Alpha and Theta.

Alpha and Theta are terms used in psychology to represent the various states of the mind when recording the brain waves. Alpha and Theta are probably the best states for relaxation, hypnotherapy, subliminal persuasion, and auto-suggestion. It's the state of mind just before we go to sleep or just after we have woken up. We can add to this our experience of pendulum dowsing.

There are four main frequencies that have been categorised: Beta, Alpha, Theta and Delta. Beta brain waves are associated with normal physical and mental activities whilst awake. Alpha waves are associated with deep relaxation, ideal for crystal dowsing. Theta waves are associated with dreaming, meditation and the experience of entering or coming out of sleep. The slowest and deepest, Delta waves, are associated with dreamless sleep, a somnambulist state.

Nature and sleep

It's said that only the fittest will survive, and because there's ruthless competition for limited resources, our planet could easily be described as a dangerous place to be. Yet the most spectacularly successful species of them all, human beings, spend almost a third of their lives paralysed and senseless - and no, I am not talking about after a good night out; I am talking about sleep.

Strange how the most advanced animals, normally watchful, shrewd and alert, drop their defences to sleep. It must mean that there's a huge benefit for all of us in sleep, or surely the powerful forces behind nature would have eliminated sleep a long time ago. Although it may have been risky sometimes to sleep, it must mean sleep is very valuable. So take a leaf out of nature's book: be as relaxed as possible when using your crystal pendulum for dowsing.

Gaining knowledge from hypnosis
In the phenomenon of hypnotism, as it is understood psychologically, there are numerous situations in which our senses are deceived by what the mind is directed to see, feel or hear during an extreme state of suggestibility.

Follow my thinking here, because I believe that, by looking at the crystal dowsing phenomena from a different angle - science and psychology - you will gain a further 'knowing'.

We have often witnessed stage hypnotists demonstrating, for example, that if they suggest to a subject that an ordinary coin being held in the hand is getting red-hot, immediately the coin will be dropped, because the person involved will say he felt his fingers being burned. Such examples of 'mind over matter', as they are called, are really commonplace in psychology.

Hypnotism was used in the beginning in surgery. It was suggested to the person that he was insensitive to pain. Hypnotism was employed very successfully for surgical anaesthesia before the discovery of ether. Can you see just how powerful the forces are that are at work here? Turn it on its head, and you'll see the kind of power that's working through the pendulum.

Chevreul's Pendulum
Michel Eugene Chevreul (1786 -1889) was a French chemist, a director at the Natural History Museum in Paris, and a man noted for his extensive researches.

He investigated mediums and clairvoyants, and the apparently inexplicable movements of the pendulums that they used to use. By a series of experiments, Chevreul proved that although people could have been acting in all good faith, the movements of the pendulum were actually caused by almost imperceptible muscular movements of the hand holding the thread; in other words, although the subjects were completely unaware of the unconscious movements of their hands, the pendulum's movements were caused by involuntary movements on the part of the individual holding the pendulum.

You can now turn this fact to your advantage, because it means the movements must be coming from the subconscious - your inner wisdom - and not the intellect, the conscious.

Mystery and Imagination

I have used this 'knowing' effect quite spectacularly at my party plan demonstrations when we are having 'an evening of mystery and imagination'. To make a point, I use the description in my book 'Wish Kit' to demonstrate this 'knowing' by using a pendulum. I tell my volunteer to hold a pendulum in their hands, and, whatever they do, not to move, but, using only the power of their mind, to imagine the pendulum moving in any direction they want. And when it does, they think it's spooky.

Is it spooky?

You should by now realise it isn't spooky, but quite natural, although at parties you can cut the atmosphere with a knife! In fact, the volunteer will often drop the pendulum and even move away from it.

It's all in the state of mind.

**"Your intelligence is always with you, overseeing your body, even though you may not be aware of its works.
Rumi (1207 -1273)**

A journey to wholeness

As we begin to trust and integrate our new-found knowledge - a gift from the spirit within - we will gradually find that if we are growing, we need to use tools, such as crystal pendulums for dowsing, less and less. We start to become increasingly secure in a profound sense of our inner 'knowing' of a sense of rightness, of well-being, of tuning into an inner peace. We find ourselves naturally and intuitively choosing to do what our bodies, minds and spirits need to do, for stimulation and to guide us to inner contentment. We then find ourselves celebrating in self-expression and fulfilment, in the sure knowledge of our spirit's existence and its purpose.

**"Live the journey,
the journey is Life"**

Crystal Healing

Fact or Fiction?
Real or Imaginary?

Why not judge for yourself!

By
Robert W. Wood D.Hp
(Diploma in Hypnotherapy

Rosewood Publishing

BK6

**Nature's crystals: a fascinating, wonderful world of shapes determined by their atomic structure.
Can there be a more spectacular sight than water when it's in the form of a snowflake crystal?**

Crystal healing - fact, or fiction?

Everybody's heard stories about crystal healing. There was the woman who was given a crystal to help her bad knee and then found, to her amazement, that her knee miraculously got better. Or people who can't sleep, who find that placing an Amethyst under their pillow seems to make them sleep like logs. Would you believe headaches can just seem to vanish? That'll be a Rose Quartz. Women becoming pregnant after years of trying – ask them how, and they'll say it was a Moonstone. Eyesight improving – that'll be Obsidian Snowflake. Memory improving – Rhodonite. Need to boost your confidence? – then try a Tiger's Eye, a beautiful stone from South Africa.

You could bring back the joys of spring with a Sodalite; and if you place a Sodalite with a Rhodonite in a glass of water, it produces the 'elixir of life', said to rejuvenate and produce youthfulness. Aches and pains? Then what you need is a Rose Quartz and Hematite combined. It's said they work wonders on aches and pains. Maybe you would like a little 'peace of mind'? Then try Green Aventurine, Rose Quartz and Rhodonite. Not feeling too good? Then the 'Healer' could be just what the doctor ordered: Carnelian, Red Jasper and Rock Crystal. And there are many more, so whatever the problem, there'll be a crystal that can help.

For many years I have researched, pondered, studied and even demonstrated crystal healing, in front of well over one hundred thousand people. One of the interesting questions I am sometimes asked after a forty-five minute presentation - often by somebody holding a crystal in their hands and about to buy it - is: "But what do I do with it?" I find this curious when I have just spent three-quarters of an hour explaining.

At the same time the vast majority seem to know what to do; they don't need to ask. So why do the majority seem to know, and yet a tiny minority don't?

Over the years I have read many books, reports, and articles. I have searched the Internet and have seen and heard volumes of stories about the effectiveness of crystals, especially with regard to healing. But more importantly, I have done my research out in the field, in front of hundreds of groups drawn from a wide range of organisations and including people from all walks of life. In short, I have served an apprenticeship.

One of my observations over the years has got to be that men are more cynical than women. However, there is a kind of hush that settles down over the men once I am into my presentation. I think it's because the men are surprised to hear, in words, what women seem to already know intuitively.
Another observation is that academics find it almost impossible to accept esoteric, new-age philosophy. Most of the books I have read by academics on this subject all seem to take great delight in rubbishing the subject and dismissing it out of hand.

Can you see the obvious?
Here's a little story to make my point:
Sherlock Holmes and Dr. Watson go camping. During the night, Holmes wakes his friend. "Watson, look up at the sky and tell me, what do you see?" And Watson says, "I see a million stars."
Holmes asks, "What does that tell you?"
The good doctor thinks about it and says, "Theologically, I can see that God is all-powerful. Astronomically, it tells me there are a million galaxies. Astrologically, I observe that Saturn is in Leo. Meteorologically, I suspect tomorrow will be a beautiful day. Horologically, I deduce that it is 2.30 am. What does it tell you, Holmes?"
"Watson, my dear friend," said the great detective, "it tells me someone has stolen our tent."

Ask any academic if he or she believes in God, and here you will find your first problem when they ask you to define what you mean by the word 'God'.

Could there be more than one truth?

Ask someone to take a ride on a big dipper at a fun fair, and then ask another to watch. Then ask them both to describe a 'big dipper' to someone else who wouldn't have a clue as to what one is. Although they would be describing the same ride, they will give two different versions. It wouldn't even matter if you put both of them onto the ride at the same time, you will still get two different versions.

Over the years I have come across many people who are walking around today, who will swear blind that a crystal or a crystal healer cured them of whatever problems, illness or troubles they had.

Divided opinions.

There are divided opinions, it's true to say. These range from the total non-believers to those who do believe, leaving the majority firmly in the middle, not knowing what to believe.

The author of this book started out thinking it would probably all be rubbish, just like having fairies at the bottom of the garden. (Sorry, if you believe in fairies.) But I quickly learned it might not be rubbish, and in fact I now firmly believe that for many, under certain circumstances, crystal healing actually does seem to work. I suggest you keep an open mind. You will be the judge and jury. First let me present some interesting points of view - but do remember it's you who will decide in the end.

To be fair, if the claims made by some were true, that crystals, lucky charms; amulets and healing stones are so effective, then common sense should tell us that nobody would be ill or emotionally upset ever again. Everybody would be wearing or carrying their own range of crystals around with them, because they would have discovered their very own panacea. Some could argue that because so many people do wear gemstones, crystals, lucky charms and amulets, they must work, or why else would people wear them? A simple answer could be that people hope they'll work, or even that they are wearing them just as a fashion item because, quite simply, they like them.

A hidden code.

What if there is another explanation? What if it's not the stones or crystals after all, but a belief in them? And if this were true, then the healing mechanism would have to be triggered more from within, rather than from without. Jesus Christ, the most famous of all healers, often spoke in a coded language before he performed a healing. Here are just a few examples - see if you can spot the code.

"Go! It will be done just as you believed it would," and his servant was healed at that very hour. *Matthew 8 -13*

Then he touched their eyes and said, "According to your faith will it be done to you." *Matthew 9 -29*

"If you have faith as small as a mustard seed, you can say to this mountain, move from here to there, and it will move. Nothing will be impossible for you." *Matthew 17 - 20*

"If you believe, you will receive whatever you ask for in prayer." *Matthew 21- 22*

"If you can," said Jesus. "Everything is possible for him who believes." Immediately the boy's father explained, "I do believe; help me overcome my unbelief!" *Mark 9 - 23*

"Daughter, your faith has healed you." *Luke. 8 - 48*

Hearing this, Jesus said to Jairus, "Don't be afraid; just believe, and she will be healed." *Luke. 8 - 50*

Are you getting the idea? And no, I'm not getting religious; it's just that if you can understand the code, you can start to understand 'healing'. I am not asking you to abandon your own powers of discrimination or personal intuitions in favour of a blind belief. Genuine knowledge and wisdom does not come from gullibility, but it comes from a deep questioning within, until the seeker has genuinely found his or her own answers.

Mother Nature.

In the past, man seems to have lived more in peace and harmony with Mother Nature and easily accepted earth's abundant treasures. You could say, man's first medicine chest was provided by Mother Earth, in the form of herbs, flowers and fruits, crystals, minerals and rocks.

We have advanced so far with technology and scientific achievement today, that it almost beggars belief just how far we seem to have travelled in such a short period of time. The effects that we enjoy have been of such enormous value and benefit to us all, and we may be so much in awe of it all that we may find ourselves forgetting our past.

oOo

A Lapidary or The History of Pretious Stones
with cautions for the undeceiving of all those that deal
with Pretious Stones.
by Thomas Nichols. Sometime of Jesus Colledge in Cambridge.
Printed by Thomas Buck Printer to the Universitie 1652

Surely, we live not in the most unknowing times of the world, nay, never was this part of the World fuller of knowledge than now it is wherein many are blest with excellent gifts and endowments by which they are enabled to enquire more thoroughly into the nature and causes of things.

oOo

Remembering who we are and where we have come from will help us to marry the valid 'old' knowledge to the 'new'. This will help us to gain a deeper understanding of ourselves, and to be in contact with our inner 'knowing'. With this thought in mind, if we study mankind from as far back as the days of the legendary lost city of Atlantis and the ancient Mayan and Hebrew civilisations, including native American as well as far Eastern cultures, we will find that throughout these ages, gemstones and crystals have been used in spiritual rituals, as aids to help with physical healing, and to help reduce stress and anxiety.

The road to Damascus.
When I first came across gemstone and crystal healing, I really thought this was more of a wind-up, put about by a few hippies who could only be described as crackpots. To be fair, they didn't do their cause any good by always looking spaced-out and saying, 'Peace, man!' - and if this is how you think, or if you think gemstone crystals are only lumps of rock, then all I ask is that you keep an open mind. If you had told me in 1993, when I first started my research, that I would become a strong advocate for crystal healing, then I would not have believed it.

In America there are many surgeons who believe that a patient's convalescence is reduced by as much as a third when crystals are used in surgery. Although these surgeons admit they don't know why this should be, they accept it as a fact and always make sure that there are crystals in the operating theatre.

Hospitals throughout the world - certainly the more enlightened ones - have taken note of the apparent therapeutic power of crystals, and so crystals can often be found at and around various points in hospitals.

Be alert.
Do not accept blindly what you are told. I never have. Always verify for yourself, if you can; check the results that have been obtained by others who have used crystals. I personally have seen, heard and experienced some amazing stories regarding gemstone and crystal healing. I think for you, the reader, we will need to go to a deeper level of understanding. We need to build a case. We need to 'put some meat onto the bones'.

A deeper level.
Quartz crystals and gemstones have always been highly prized for their beauty, and also for their renowned healing and spiritual properties. They have been associated with healers, shamans, priests, spiritual seekers and many others who have all used these so-called 'special powers'.

Science has yet to discover what is actually going on during crystal healing, and only by trying out a healing system for ourselves are we able to judge its worth. It may surprise you to find that real changes are clearly felt, and lasting benefits are clearly gained, by many participants who have used crystals.

A very interesting fact about crystals is that they grow, and continue to grow until all the free atoms are arranged. A crystal may have remained the same for thousands or even millions of years, but crystals do actually grow in the ground in a 'matrix' (this is a rock in which fossils, pebbles etc are embedded).

A little science.

Quartz crystals absorb, use and store energy, and mature, just like anything else in existence that we consider to be 'alive'. When subjected to outside force, such as light, pressure, heat or electricity, quartz crystals quickly restore themselves to their original internal stability, this stability being the quality that makes them so important in modern day technology.

We find crystals are used in watches - you must have heard of 'quartz watches'. Put on a CD player and you will have activated a sound system that uses a laser to read tiny pits and flat spots from a plastic coated metal disc. That laser uses a ruby crystal - and this explains why the laser is red.

We can find crystals being used as switching and regulating devices in engines - engines that power everything from cars to space shuttles. Your car radio uses a transistor made from a silicon quartz crystal. So we are using crystals every day in the form of computer chips, liquid crystal displays, transistors, clocking devices ... and there are many more.

Did you know that the most common element on earth is oxygen? and the second most common is silicon? So it won't be a surprise to find the most common of crystals is silicon quartz, a crystal that grows from the combination of silicon and oxygen. That is why they say computer chips come from Silicon Valley.

Colour:
When other factors become involved, such as natural inclusions or background radiation, then the characteristics of the quartz start to change enough for it to appear coloured or smoky. This factor very cleverly links crystals to their best use, for healing, because colour is used as a primary identification for gemstones and crystals.

Amazingly, if a few atoms from another element become included within the lattice structure of the quartz molecules whilst the crystal is forming, or if another mineral crystallizes within the quartz as it grows, it becomes distorted. This distortion helps to explain why there are so many coloured varieties of quartz.

Colour therapy.

To reach a deeper understanding of crystal healing, you will find it useful if we now explore colour therapy. Colour therapy, like gemstones and crystals, can be an effortless system of treatment that can help with illness, pain and tiredness. It can help us to look and feel younger and enable us to enjoy life with more energy, vigour and vitality. All this can be achieved by simply using the mind to 'experience' colours.

Our brain governs the healing and well-being process in our bodies. Indian yoga has identified seven energy centres, the 'Chakra' system, which all must be balanced for good health. What we are interested in here is energy - the healing energy. Colour, as an indicator, is one of the characteristics of energy; it's called 'frequency'.

More colour science.

Colour is a function of light. It is determined by the frequency of the light wave as observed by the human eye. The visible light spectrum goes from the lowest frequency, red, to the highest, violet. This spectrum is, in order: Red, Orange, Yellow, Green, Blue, Indigo and Violet. My way of remembering it when I was at school was: Richard Of York Gained Battles In Vain. In case you didn't already know, these are the seven colours of the rainbow, in their correct order.

Mankind's effort to heal with light is as old as recorded history. The foundation of modern colour therapy rests with seventeenth century scientists including Sir Isaac Newton (1642 -1727) and his famous prism tests. He was the first to show that 'white light' is a mixture of all colours of the visible spectrum. He proved that when the seven-colour band was passed through a prism, the colours re-combined to form 'white light'.

Others have taken this work further, and quite successfully explored colours and their effects in healing. Gemstones and crystals are easily identified by their colour, and this gives us a general guide to the frequencies on which they operate, and a link with their energy.

Healing energy - frequencies.

The body also has 'frequencies' of energy waves. Some have been accurately measured by Western science; some haven't. However, just because science hasn't figured out how to measure them all, this doesn't mean they don't exist.

Crystal therapy makes use of this energy system within the body. So in crystal healing, one of the first things to consider is the colour frequency.

There are specific areas of the body that are main centres for the flow of energy. In Sanskrit, they're called Chakras. (Sanskrit is an ancient language of India - in fact it is the oldest recorded member of the Indo branch of the Indo-European family of languages.) These energy centres correspond to frequencies, low to high. The lowest-frequency energy centre is the first Chakra.

If you start to consider all of this intuitively, you will realise that the first Chakra is at the base of the spine. The next six are located in order, starting at the reproductive organs; then the navel area; the heart; the base of the throat; the brow; and finally at the crown of the head. The colours that represent these Chakras are roughly the frequencies that represent red to violet, lowest to highest.

So we are now establishing a very basic rule of thumb for the use of gemstones and crystals. Deep red stones such as Jasper or deeper Rose Quartz would resonate with the lower Chakras, and violet to clear, represented by Amethyst and Rock Crystal, would be associated with the higher ones.

Robert's research.
Years ago now, when I first started researching into the mysteries surrounding gemstones and crystals, I had chosen a Red Jasper for the star sign Aries. You'll have to read my book 'Discover Why Crystal Healing Works' for a full explanation, but briefly - I wanted to find an authentic list of birthstones. I read and researched many different sources of information, and eventually decided to take the 'mean average', mainly because all my sources seemed to be saying something different. No two of the lists I was researching were saying the same thing. So I thought that if the majority were saying that Red Jasper was the stone for Aries, then that was good enough for me. This was how I acquired my unique list of twelve birthstones.

Gemstones Crystals and the Bible.
In my early days of research I used to pass around baskets full of tumblestones, and ask my audience to pick out a stone they liked. I was trying to establish whether there was a connection between birthstones and ourselves.

I didn't think there would be; but to my amazement it seemed that there was, because many people seemed to pick out their own birthstone. Sometimes as many as 70% did. I also researched into connections between gemstones or crystals and the Bible,; because a friend had told me that the gemstones and crystals I was researching could be found there.

Amazingly I seemed to find information was starting to flood in from all kinds of sources. Some seemed, at the time, very strange. I found people sent me information through the post, especially after they had heard me give my talk. They would write and say things like, "I hope this will help in your research." It felt as if I was being sent pieces of a jigsaw, and although at the time it felt odd it's surprising just how well all those pieces seem to have fitted together.

I noticed that passages from books were starting to stand out, but the strangest of all was when a bible I was looking at seemed to open up and I was drawn to a story in Exodus (28-15) relating to twelve stones. Strange, because at the time I was engaged in trying to find twelve authentic birthstones.

It became even stranger when, on the same day that I came across this story in Exodus, I found myself being drawn to a story in the New Testament entitled 'A New Jerusalem' (Revelation 21-19). When you consider that there are nearly one thousand four hundred pages in a Bible, with only two lists of twelve stones anywhere, and I seemed somehow to have found both lists on the same day, it is even more mystifying. Was this a coincidence, or what? Curiously, this other list of twelve stones representing a New Jerusalem said that the first foundation was a Jasper. This was the same stone I had chosen for the birth sign Aries, which can be called the first foundation in Astrology and is the first one described in the Chakras.

Revelation 21-19.
The sixth foundation of this New Jerusalem was Carnelian; the sixth star sign in astrology is Virgo, and its stone is a Carnelian. If ever the pieces of a jigsaw came together, they were doing so now! The twelfth and final foundation was Amethyst; in astrology, the last is Pisces; the birthstone selected was the same, Amethyst; and to cap it all, in the colours of the Chakra the last one, and the highest colour which is visible to the eye, is violet - Amethyst.

Colour therefore proved to be a very important consideration in the concept of crystal healing. Now, whilst colour may be important, other factors are too, because gemstones and crystals have an evolutionary history as well; that is, each stone or crystal over the years has attracted its own unique kind of 'providence'.

One of the qualities that typifies traditional healing arts, alternative therapies etc, is the respect for the 'holistic' nature of our existence: that the whole may be greater than the sum of its parts. You cannot work with one and ignore the other. The surgeon can repair an ulcer but the wise man looks for the reason behind the illness.

Healing Energy.
The healing energy which I mentioned earlier is not isolated. It is connected with the energy that is in all things. We are a part of a holistic event: the Universe. One of the defining characteristics of traditional alternative therapies is the respect for, and awareness of, our natural healing energy - the life force built within. In Chinese it's known as 'chi'. The Ayuruedic system, handed down through 7,500-year-old Vedic texts of India, defines three basic energies: pitta, vata and kapha. The Christians refer to the Father, the Son and the Holy Spirit. The indigenous tribe of the Kalahari refer to the healing power of nature as 'num'. There is not an ancient culture you can think of that doesn't acknowledge this natural connection with healing energy. So - healing energy, we now know, has certain characteristics. Learn how to acknowledge, honour and use this energy, for it is the key to healing. Gemstones and crystals are an important part of that key - use them.

The following information is a fluid interpretation from many sources.
Any information given in this book is not intended to be taken as a replacement for medical advice. Any person with a condition requiring medical attention should consult a qualified doctor or therapist.

RED JASPER A powerful healing stone. Can help those suffering from emotional problems; its power to give strength and console such sufferers is well known. Good for: kidneys, bladder. Improves the sense of smell.

ROSE QUARTZ Healing qualities for the mind. Gives help with migraine and headaches. Good for: spleen, kidneys and circulatory system. Coupled with Hematite, works wonders on aches and pains throughout the body.

BLACK ONYX Can give a sense of courage, and helps to discover truth. Instils calm and serenity. Good for: bone marrow, relief of stress.

MOTHER OF PEARL Aptly dubbed the sea of tranquillity. Calms the nerves. Good for: calcified joints, digestive system.

TIGER EYE The 'confidence stone'. Inspires brave but sensible behaviour. Good for: liver, kidneys, bladder. Invigorates and energises.

CARNELIAN A very highly-evolved healer, good for: rheumatism, depression, neuralgia. Helps regularise the menstrual cycle.

GREEN AVENTURINE Stabilises through inspiring independence. Acts as a general tonic. Good for: skin conditions; losing anxiety and fears.

RHODONITE Improves the memory; reduces stress. Good for: emotional trauma, mental breakdown; spleen, kidneys, heart and blood.

SODALITE Imparts youth and freshness. Calms and clears the mind. When combined with Rhodonite, can produce the 'Elixir of Life'.

OBSIDIAN SNOWFLAKE A powerful healer. Brings insight and understanding, wisdom and love. Good for: eyesight, stomach and intestines.

BLUE AGATE Improves the ego. A stone of strength and courage: a supercharger of energy. Good for: stress, certain ear disorders.

AMETHYST Aids creative thinking. Relieves insomnia when placed under pillow. Good for; blood pressure, fits, grief and insomnia.

HEMATITE A very optimistic inspirer of courage and magnetism. Lifts gloominess. Good for: blood, spleen; generally strengthens the body.

ROCK CRYSTAL Enlarges the aura of everything near to it and acts as a catalyst to increase the healing powers of other minerals. Good for: brain, soul; dispels negativity in your own energy field.

MOONSTONE Gives inspiration and enhances the emotions. Good for: period pain and kindred disorders, fertility and childbearing.

Power Gems.
Now here is a list of the most popular Power Gems, this time taking the desired effect, rather than the gemstones and crystals, as our the starting point. Using our unique knowledge, we have created the following combinations from the 15 gemstones and crystals previously listed.

For example, someone wanting to know the luckiest stones can look at 'Good Luck'. To find out the most powerful healing crystals, then look at 'Healer'. If you want the stones best suited to everyday ailments, then 'To Remove Aches & Pains' are the ones for you. Feeling under the weather? - then try 'To Lift Depression'; or if you're trying to lose weight or give up smoking, then try 'For Willpower'.

This range has been designed so that you don't have to guess which stones do what. In this day and age, some may take all this as no more than a little fun; but remember, years ago they didn't have chemists as we know them today, and this is what people used: gemstones and crystals.

The most powerful combination of crystals discovered for healing:
HEALER - Carnelian, Red Jasper and Rock Crystal.

Three of the best-known Gemstones for attracting Good Luck:
GOOD LUCK - Obsidian Snowflake, Green Aventurine and Moonstone.

To capture 'stillness in movement', to attract harmony and tranquillity:
PEACE OF MIND - Green Aventurine, Rose Quartz and Rhodonite.

Stones and crystals to help us acquire willpower
FOR WILLPOWER - Rose Quartz, Black Onyx and Rock Crystal.

Combined to create the most imaginative aphrodisiac. Very sensuous:
ADULTS ONLY - Rose Quartz, Amethyst and Carnelian.

Help to ease aches and pains including headaches and tensions:
TO REMOVE ACHES & PAINS - Rose Quartz, Hematite & Rock Crystal.

To preserve youth and retards the aging process:
ELIXIR OF LIFE - Rhodonite and Sodalite.

Gemstones to help boost energy and vitality, to help invigorate:
ENERGY BOOSTER - Carnelian, Amethyst and Rock Crystal.

Designed for that special purpose, to reach a deeper level of mind:
IMAGINE - Rose Quartz, Amethyst and Green Aventurine.

To help nature along when starting a family:
FERTILITY - Moonstone, Rose Quartz and Rock Crystal.

See your local stockist for any Gemstones and Crystals mentioned in this publication. However, if you are having difficulty in obtaining any of the stones mentioned, we do offer our own mail order service and would be more than pleased to supply any of the stones listed.

Most Gemstones and Crystals, with just a few exceptions (eg Mother of Pearl), can be supplied in the form of Tumblestones. These are smooth, rounded stones, ideal as a Birthstone or as Healing Crystals. The nature of Mother of Pearl, and one or two others, prevents them being supplied as Tumblestones; however, we would be pleased to supply these in their natural form.

For further details - write to:
Rosewood, P.O. Box 219. Huddersfield, West Yorkshire. HD2 2YT

Email:- info@rosewood-gifts.co.uk

www.rosewood-gifts.co.uk

How to
Activate the
Hidden Power
In
Gemstones and
Crystals

By
Robert W. Wood D.Hp
(Diploma in Hypnotherapy)

Rosewood Publishing

BK7

The most powerful word for 'healing' on earth

'We can see and feel the rays of the sun
but not the power that created it.'

With time, help and patience,
we are learning to see the unseen,
to hear and understand that which cannot be heard,
and to speak that which is unspoken.

Our fascination with Gemstones and Crystals

How often I've heard people say, "But what do I do with them?" I answer: "You have to connect with them." "But how?" So this book is dedicated to answering that question: "How?" Our journey starts at the very beginning. It's only here that we will discover how this fascination with Gemstones and Crystals started, and where the information came from.

It began...

Starting at the beginning means going back in time to the creation of planet Earth and our solar system. Earth was formed around 4,500 million years ago, and all the building blocks of the Universe are captured here on Earth. Our Earth is over 80% 'crystal', the crust being largely silicon and oxygen; and, when combined with six common elements - Sodium, Aluminium, Calcium, Iron, Magnesium and Potassium - this 'chemical cocktail' helped to produce the building blocks for our world. With this cocktail came an amazing variety of Gemstones and Crystals in all kinds of shapes, sizes and colours.

What are Crystals?

They are of mineral substance, and their molecular composition is arranged and geometrically fixed. When you look at a crystal you can see many different sides or 'faces', angles, planes and points. The word 'crystal' comes from the Greek word 'krystallos' meaning 'ice'. The Greeks gave the name believing that crystals were ice, frozen. Crystalline materials as diverse as sugar, metal, salt - even our teeth - have all got one thing in common: an ordered internal structure of a regularly-repeating three-dimensional pattern. Even the most irregular or misshapen crystal shares this atomical neatness. A crystal's external shape is dependent on its specific chemical ingredients, the way the atoms are linked together, and the conditions prevailing at the time of growth. There are many different permutations, producing a wide variation in shapes, colour and hardness.

Colour.

The majority of crystals contain 'rogue' atoms - minute impurities, usually metal, within their chemical structure. These trace elements, or impurities, contribute to the wide range of colours. As a general rule of thumb: the greater the amount of trace impurities contained within the crystal, the deeper the colour. There are some crystals, such as agate and jasper, which we call Gemstones. These contain the same atomic structure, but, unlike crystal, their form is not visible to the naked eye and they appear to be ordinary coloured stones without geometric form, just like pebbles from a beach. Only by using a microscope is it possible to see the thousands of little crystals of which they are composed.

Crystal electricity.

Certain crystals, most notably the Quartz family, can convert mechanical pressure into electrical energy. To demonstrate this, take two quartz crystals - rock crystal, rose quartz or amethyst will do - and rub them together in the dark. You'll see them light up quite spectacularly. It's called a 'piezoelectric' effect, from the Greek word 'piezo' meaning 'I press'. If you have a gas oven you may have used a special lighter-wand to create a spark. This special tool has a piece of quartz built into it, which releases energy (the spark) when it is used, and it works without the need of a battery. While natural quartz is abundant, it is rarely perfect, with all its 'rogue' trace elements rendering it unsuitable for commercial use. So piezoelectric crystals are produced synthetically in the laboratory.

Although synthetic, they still have the same atomic structure and properties as their natural counterparts.

A Quartz Watch.

Why is there a quartz in a watch? The answer is, because quartz makes a timepiece so accurate, to within only a second or two a year - and that's accurate. So how does it work? Scientists discovered that the atoms within a micro-thin slice of synthetic quartz (such as is ideal for clocks and watches) vibrate at 32,768 times per second. The crystal requires very little power, and this is often supplied by a very tiny battery. As the atoms in the quartz vibrate they emit very precise electronic pulses. These pulses are then channelled through microchip circuitry, where they are successively halved in a series of 15 steps. The result is really astounding: it produces a single, constant pulse per second. Which is why watches and clocks are now so accurate.

From science to the 'mysteries'.

Even earliest man found gemstones and crystals attractive and colourful, and used them for jewellery; but at the same time there was another interest developing, and this more to do with their 'magical attraction', rather than their looks. It's not difficult to understand their fascination, when you think about the piezoelectric effect: stones that light up.

I think it's strange that even to-day, things don't seem to have changed that much. On one hand we have the geologists, who will drool over a lovely piece of crystal and talk about its shape, its symmetry, its inclusions and how it looks. On the other hand, we have the New Age followers - crystal healers and the alternative therapists - all drooling over the same piece and explaining how it feels, describing its energy, its power and what it can do.

A mystical journey, a brief history.

In pre-historic times, people were nomadic, always on the move. Then about 6000 years ago, early man began to settle down and build himself more permanent homes, and he started keeping animals and growing crops. These early civilisations, such as the Babylonians, Egyptians and Chinese, began to believe that the stars and planets that they could see so clearly in the night skies, influenced their lives. The Babylonians, in particular, thought that the position of the stars represented coded messages from the gods.

Their priests, holy men and sages spent much of their time studying these so-called messages with great care, observing and plotting the night sky. Studying in this way produced a science that we now know as Astrology.

The Egyptian Connection.

Here's a mystery that won't go away. The Egyptians have had a love affair for thousands of years with the brightest star in the sky. It's called 'Sirius', and according to their mythology it represents their goddess Isis. The great pyramid at Gizeh was believed to have been built because of an ancient knowledge connecting planet Earth with the Sirius star system, often referred to as the Dog Star. In the pyramid it's been discovered that there are various chambers or rooms. These have been named the Kings, the Queens and the Lower Chambers. These chambers have tiny passages, like windows, leading to the outside of the pyramid; and on rare occasions, at intervals which may stretch across thousands of years, there are times when, if you were in the chamber looking out, you would witness a perfect alignment with various star systems, including the star Sirius. What it all means still remains a mystery.

Spaceships.
Some Chinese stone discs were discovered, and when the inscriptions on them were translated, they told of a crashed spaceship from the same star system Sirius. Even more curious is a unique ceremony practised only by the African tribe, Dogon. They tell the legend of the Nommos, who arrived in a vessel along with fire and thunder. The Nommos could live on land, but dwelled mostly in the sea. Similar creatures have been noted in other ancient civilisations, including Egypt's goddess Isis.

The African Tribe - Dogon.
It seems that the Dogon tribe knew a lot about the star system Sirius, including the existence of a smaller star called Sirius B. Both these are well outside our own solar system, and it's impossible to see the smaller star with the naked eye; so this begs the question: How did they know? A photo of this smaller star was not obtained until 1970. Yet the Dogon tribe had revealed their knowledge of the Sirius star system to a French anthropologist in 1930. It's even been suggested that this information is more than 5000 years old and was possessed by the ancient Egyptians before 3200 BC - well before the Pyramids. The Dogon also claimed that a third star existed in the Sirius system, and around it orbited a planet from which the Nommos came. This Sirius mystery has now changed dramatically. Why? Because in the year 1995 two French astronomers, Daniel Benest and J.L. Duvent, published the results of years of study, and for the very first time confirmed the existence of this third star.

Six thousand years ago, ancient man had a knowledge that modern man is only just rediscovering.

Rather than go deeper into the unknown,
let's discover what we do know.

Cause and Effect.

Can a lump of rock really do anything? Can it heal, change luck, and give more energy? The simple answer, you may be surprised to know, is: Yes, it can. There is a 'law of cause and effect'; this is the underpinning bedrock of the Universe. It's also a very useful protector whenever you come across something you can't understand or explain, because you know that there is an explanation, even if you can't see one at the time. Understanding this gives you control over your mind, but especially your imagination.

Let's not look at 'if they can', but more 'how they can'. We often see the effect; let's look for the cause.

You wouldn't dream of entering a room at night without first putting the light on. The power's there; you just need to turn it on. Using this analogy: if the lights didn't go on (that's the 'effect'), what could be the cause? It could be that the light bulb is broken. Solution: change it. Or it could be that you haven't paid the bill and have been cut off: pay it. Now turn this around. You need a light bulb that's working - your 'crystal'; the electricity to be on - 'the hidden power'; and someone to switch it on - 'you'.

Expand your mind.

Who could believe that an aeroplane full of passengers, loaded with tons of fuel, could fly? It seems impossible - but it does. Or that a ship made out of steel can float? But it does. It's impossible; but it does. We now believe it because we see it; and because we can see it, we believe it. Now imagine, for a moment, that you didn't know about planes, and all you could see was the vapour trail in the sky.

Without the mental anchor of 'cause and effect', what would your mind, and especially your imagination, make of it? It would run riot. You would feel anxious, nervous - not understanding causes unease; but the moment someone says, "That's an aeroplane you're looking at, they take off and land at airports," - the fact that someone else seems to know what an aeroplane is, can be quite reassuring. And so knowledge, wherever it comes from, moves us from a state of anxiety to calm and serenity.

A solid foundation.

How did we get from earth science into a world of 'magic'? What happened? The answer is, 'Man' happened. It is only Man who can take an abstract and work with it. He is responsible for adding the one ingredient that's so powerful, it can't and won't be held back; nothing on earth can stop it; and one day it may be shown that it is the very reason for life itself.

In the beginning was the word, and the word was with God, through him all things were made; without him nothing was made that has been made. Then the word became flesh and lived.

Is the Genie out of the bottle? Let me tell you not what it is, but where it is. What you are discovering forms the first step towards activating your crystals. This is the first foundation of your knowledge: that which we are seeking will be found in the 'mind' - but where in the mind? It's in the part called the 'subconscious'. Before I tell you where in the subconscious, let me show you, using words and pictures, your subconscious.

The subconscious.

First of all, the good news is that we all have a subconscious, because we all have a mind. Whether we choose to use it or not mainly depends on ourselves. Our minds are likened to the most powerful computers on earth, and it's nobody's fault except our own if we choose not to use it. In my mind it's a free gift from the Creator and it's ours to use. Some may say, "But my brain isn't any good, I failed at school." I promise you it is, especially for what you are about to discover.

There are two main parts to the brain, our mind. One's the conscious, and the other the subconscious. The conscious acts like a 'gatekeeper'. It controls what is allowed in. Imagine the largest stately home in the world, set in thousands of acres, employing tens of thousands of people from all walks of life and backgrounds - and the only access is past the gatekeeper. That's how the mind works. Another analogy could be the captain of the world's largest ship - the captain representing the conscious, and all the workers below decks representing the subconscious. Sadly, if the captain decided to run aground, the crew wouldn't stop him.

It's important to bear this in mind. The power to direct is in the conscious part, but the power to achieve is held within the subconscious. So make sure they're both going in the right direction.

When two or more are together I am there. I tell you that if two of you on earth agree about anything you ask for, it will be done for you by my Father in Heaven.

MATT. 18: 19-20

The greatest computer of then all.
Those of you who can drive a car will understand this. When you can drive, you 'consciously' decide where you are going - "I'm going from here to there" - but you cannot drive a car 'consciously'. You drive it 'automatically'; that is, through the subconscious. If you want to know what I mean, just look at a learner trying to drive a car consciously, having to think about the clutch, handbrake, mirrors, signals and brakes. When they are thinking about it, it's difficult and awkward. But the moment the subconscious kicks in, not only can they drive using all the instruments available, they are also able to read the road, see dangers and possible problems and at the same time compute situations that may never arise; and all this is being done every microsecond (one millionth of a second). And if that doesn't blow your mind, then think about this: while all this is happening, they are more than capable of holding a conversation. Wow! There isn't a computer on this planet that can drive a car and I don't think there ever will be. So who are we?

There is another way of showing you your subconscious other than in words, and that is with pictures. On page 120 there is a picture of a woman. Just look at it, and after a while the picture will change. This effect is your subconscious having to reveal itself; because there are two pictures in one, and basically the subconscious is saying to the conscious, "I can't make up my mind, see what you think." So the picture will continue to change backwards and forwards, forcing your subconscious to reveal itself.

The Imagination.
The power to connect to all things is within the mind, and you are now beginning to understand just how powerful your mind really is. Not only can it drive a car, but it can also transmit and receive thoughts, a little like the way the Internet works. Within the subconscious lies the greatest power of them all - the Imagination.

Once you have discovered how to turn this 'program' on - and you will - then activating the 'hidden power' in gemstones and crystals becomes child's play.

Another way of experiencing and explaining the power of imagination: have you ever gone to pick up a telephone that's been ringing, only to find yourself feeling that you somehow know who it is, and when you pick up the phone you discover you were right? It's commonly called 'telepathy' ('a communication between people of thoughts, feelings etc involving mechanisms that cannot be understood in terms of known scientific laws'). I think that it's because the person making the phone call knows you and, whilst they are dialling or thinking about dialling, they are forming an image; in other words, they are imagining you. This is probably done without thinking; but it's this image that somehow gets transmitted, and you are the one who picks up on it.

A secret code.
It doesn't matter if the person phoning lives half way around the world, you can still experience it. And what can travel so fast around the world? The Internet can. However, there is a secret code. Understand this and activating your crystal really will be 'child's play'. It's this: whenever you use your power of imagination to seek, attract, achieve, change or heal, you have to add one more ingredient, and this ingredient is vital.

I once used this formula so effectively that the results could only be described as spectacular. I bought and removed a 'mountain'. Yes, you read it right. Why a mountain? Because I thought, if I could remove it - the mountain, that is - then I might be able to build houses on the site. And I did. I removed a mountain and built houses. How did I do it? I used the same principles found in this book. You'll have to read my book 'Discover Why Crystal Healing Works' to read the full story (copies available from the publishers, their name is on the back cover). Believe me, with this vital ingredient you can move mountains; I did. And the secret is this: whenever you visualise your dream, your goal or desire, you have to add one more thing. You have to add feeling or an emotion. It makes a difference. It seems to energise the thought.

112

Jesus said, "Therefore I tell you, whatever you ask for in prayer, believe that you have received it, and it will be yours."

How do you believe you have received something? Imagine you already have it; see it in your mind's eye; and then imagine how would you feel if you did have it. The feeling helps to energise the thought. This is also a formulation for prayer. The 'power of prayer' is real; but change the expression to the 'power of thought', and the power comes back to where it should be: within each and everyone of us. It's not exclusive to a church, although you'll find it there. I did.

Imagining a feeling is not that difficult, but you do have to know the difference between seeing in your mind's eye and feeling it. How would you feel if you won the lottery, or were told by a doctor that you were expecting, after years of trying to conceive? if you found a new career, or were offered a promotion? if you were healed, or told you were in remission? It's the difference between watching an erotic film, as compared to being in it.

A coincidence.
I believe there is a coded language; so whenever I hear someone say, "You won't believe this," or, "That's strange," or, "I was just thinking about you," or, "That's a coincidence," I always listen to what comes next - because this is the hidden power at work. We have all been giving 'free will', and this allows us to dismiss this power. And how do we dismiss it? - we call it 'a coincidence'.

An example of this way of thinking is the following story: Whilst I was walking through town on a Friday afternoon, I had what I thought was a great idea. If only I could find that picture, what a lovely way to finish my talks and presentations! I called into a specialist bookshop and described this picture to them. To my relief the assistant seemed to know what I was talking about. But then the bombshell: "I know what you mean, but I haven't a clue where you'll find it," he said. So I left the shop with a feeling of disappointment. I thought at the time that it would have been a brilliant idea.

On Saturday and even Sunday I still felt this disappointment, but by Monday I seemed to have forgotten all about it. That is, until my daughter came in from work and told me how a friend of hers had been to a car boot sale the previous day and had bought what she thought was a very unusual tapestry. In fact it was so unusual that she (my daughter) tried to draw me a picture of it, because she thought I might find it interesting. When I looked, I couldn't believe my eyes. It was the same picture I had tried to find three days earlier in the specialist bookshop. Now was that a coincidence, or not?

The same picture is at the top of page three. If you haven't already noticed, the word is upside down; and if you need a clue - look into the light, not the dark, and you'll see it. It's the most powerful name on earth that I know for representing love, hope, peace and understanding, and the power to heal. I had gone into the shop, which was a Christian bookshop, and described the picture to the assistant whilst at the same time I was imagining it.

I was seeing it in my mind's eye. That's how we think: we see pictures, symbols and images. So I imagined it; then I added a feeling. In this case, surprisingly, it was a feeling of disappointment. It's this extra ingredient - a feeling - that seems to help.

Why not try out the following experiment: look at your phone and imagine it ringing. Hear the tone within your mind. Then imagine answering it, and it being someone you would like to hear from. Then imagine how would you feel if it was them. Energise it. It's this that seems to make the difference. If the person you have imagined, with feeling, lives halfway around the world and calls you, it could save you a fortune on phone bills. If you find you are good at this, and I know many people who are, then everybody will be calling you; and often when they do call they will start the conversation by saying something like "I just had this thought that I should give you a call." Try it - it works.

The hidden power.
The 'hidden power' is another name many would give to the 'Universal Life Force'. It's representative of the energy that created the Universe. Many may call it God. Like an artist - you know he existed by the pictures he painted. And where do you find the 'God' of today? You'll find him in each and every one of us. All this could be likened to making a phone call.

If you know the person's number, you can ring them anywhere in the world; all you have to do is own a phone, make sure it's turned on, and dial the number, and that's all there is to it.

Now imagine all the things that have to be in place for us to make the call. The person on the other end has to have a phone and it has to be turned on. We need the engineers and the scientists who build the systems; the satellites; the cables; the motivation, the energy and the imagination - all the ingredients that represent 'Power for life'. Discover for yourselves the hidden power. It's real and you are now learning how to activate it.

Four simple steps.
With our newly-found basic knowledge, and with the help of our wisdom and understanding, let's activate and connect with the hidden power. It's the same power that can be found in the creation of Gemstones and Crystal. Our first step is to select; the second is to cleanse; the third is to connect; and the fourth, to visualise and finally to receive.

Step one.
Start by selecting the crystal or gemstone you want. It will be the one that represents your desire, aims or goals. To help, there is a list of gemstones and crystals on page fifteen. Here you'll find the most popular gemstones and crystals, plus our own unique range of 'power gems'. These have been designed around titles, rather than stones - for example, 'Good Luck' or 'Energy Booster'. There's the 'Healer', or 'To remove aches and pains'; or you may be looking for 'Peace of Mind'. You may be thinking of an Amethyst to help you sleep, or the 'Adults Only' to keep you awake; whatever the need, there'll be a gemstone that can help.

Step two.
Next we need to clean them. Why? Because there are many who believe that stones can carry both positive and negative energy, and because you don't know where the stones have been. It won't do them any harm, so, to be safe, we clean them. It's a little like the body's DNA, but in this case it's the stone that's holding the memory. So, to neutralise any adverse effects, we cleanse them. You can, if you wish, just wash them or hold them under a running tap; I've heard of some placing them into a stream for a few minutes; you can even bury them in the ground for 24 hours to allow Mother Nature to re-energise them, and then wash them. In fact, the more you do, and the more ritualistic it is, the better they seem to work.

There are as many ways as you can imagine. In my research I have never come across a right or wrong way: just find the way that feels comfortable for you, and it will be your 'right way'.

Step three.
Next you have to connect with them. Don't be confused; this is a mental exercise. You are now going to draw upon all that 'personal computer power' that's held within the brain; you're going to focus and energise your thoughts to connect. At its simplest, you could just wear one, or carry it in your pocket or purse. You could make or buy a pouch to carry them in. My mother at a craft fair told of how she had got one of the lucky lottery stones (Green Aventurine, it's said to be a money magnet), and although she said she hadn't yet won, she found that ever since she had carried it in her purse she had never felt short of money. Since hearing this I've always carried a Green Aventurine in my pocket. Here is the point: if that stone now went missing, I would know about it. Why? Because I know I am now connected to it.

I remember at one display I lost my stone. I looked high and low for it. I even moved the furniture. Anyone watching would have thought I'd lost the Crown Jewels. Just as I was leaving I realised the only place I hadn't looked was under the piano. So I went back, moved the piano, and yes - you've guessed - the stone was there. So was I connected or not?

If you buy a Gemstone or Crystal and bring it home, put it into a drawer and forget about it, you're not connected. You have to find your way of interacting with it. If you carried a stone or crystal, and it got lost, and you didn't notice, then you were not connected. But if you did notice and started to look for it, then you were connected. Are you getting the idea? It's like the difference between a mother and a babysitter. The babysitter only connects with the child for the duration of the time she's 'sitting', whereas the mother is always connected, even when she goes out and leaves the child in the hands of the babysitter.

Step four.
Now you are connected, you have to use the greatest power of all. It's your imagination that holds the key. You now have to visualise what you want from your crystal; you have to see the end result. This is like going into a railway station and asking for a ticket. The station master will ask you where you want to go, and if you say you don't know, then you have missed the point.

However, if you can say exactly what you want, then you are really more than halfway there.

The purpose of visualisation is a little like making a phone call to a helpline that's only got an answering machine. It means you are going to do all the talking - or in this case, the 'imagining'. You hope and believe that eventually someone will listen, and will then help. The only difference is that when they do 'listen', it's not to words, but to images and thoughts: your visualisation.

For example, if you would like to become pregnant, then select a Moonstone (said to be good for childbearing and fertility), wash it, and then, whilst holding it, imagine your desired outcome. Imagine the midwife saying, "Congratulations - it's a boy!" Now here is the key: Imagine, at the same time, how would you feel if it happened. Energise the thought by adding a feeling. In church it's called the 'power of prayer', and it's real. Expect a result; in fact, be surprised if you don't get one.
Never let go or stop living in hope. You can change the future by changing the way you think. Tomorrow is still to come. Make the call, and let Universal Law take care of the rest; and be overjoyed when it does. Be prepared to receive.

Although the following information is not authoritative,
it is a fluid interpretation from many sources.
Any information given in this book is not intended to be taken as a
replacement for medical advice. Any person with a condition
requiring medical attention should consult a qualified doctor or
therapist.
On no account should a gemstone or crystal ever be swallowed.

RED JASPER A powerful healing stone. Can help those suffering from emotional problems; its power to give strength and console such sufferers is well known. Good for: kidneys, bladder. Improves the sense of smell.
ROSE QUARTZ Healing qualities for the mind. Gives help with migraine and headaches. Good for: spleen, kidneys and circulatory system. Coupled with Hematite, works wonders on aches and pains throughout the body. Lifts spirits and dispels negative thoughts.

BLACK ONYX Can give a sense of courage, and helps to discover truth. Instils calm and serenity. Good for: bone marrow, relief of stress.

MOTHER OF PEARL Aptly dubbed the sea of tranquillity. Calms the nerves. Good for: calcified joints, digestive system.

TIGER EYE The 'confidence stone'. Inspires brave but sensible behaviour. Good for: liver, kidneys, bladder. Invigorates and energises.

CARNELIAN A very highly-evolved healer. Good for: rheumatism, depression, neuralgia. Helps regularise the menstrual cycle.

GREEN AVENTURINE Stabilises through inspiring independence. Acts as a general tonic. Good for: skin conditions; losing anxiety and fears.

RHODONITE Improves the memory; reduces stress. Good for: emotional trauma, mental breakdown; spleen, kidneys, heart and blood.

SODALITE Imparts youth and freshness. Calms and clears the mind. When combined with Rhodonite, can produce the 'Elixir of Life'.

OBSIDIAN SNOWFLAKE A powerful healer. Brings insight and understanding, wisdom and love. Good for: eyesight, stomach and intestines.

BLUE AGATE Improves the ego. A stone of strength and courage; a supercharger of energy. Good for: stress, certain ear disorders.

AMETHYST Aids creative thinking. Relieves insomnia when placed under pillow. Good for: blood pressure, fits, grief and insomnia.

HEMATITE A very optimistic inspirer of courage and magnetism. Lifts gloominess. Good for: blood, spleen; generally strengthens the body.

ROCK CRYSTAL Enlarges the aura of everything near to it and acts as a catalyst to increase the healing powers of other minerals. Good for: brain, soul; dispels negativity in your own energy field.

MOONSTONE Gives inspiration and enhances the emotions. Good for: period pain and kindred disorders, fertility and childbearing.

oOo

Power Gems.
A unique group of Gemstones and Crystals, carefully linked in harmony to unite their individual mystic powers and provide a holistic force which can revive health, increase wealth, bring peace and provide energy.

HEALER - Carnelian, Red Jasper and Rock Crystal.

GOOD LUCK - Obsidian Snowflake, Green Aventurine and Moonstone.

PEACE OF MIND - Green Aventurine, Rose Quartz and Rhodonite.

FOR WILLPOWER - Rose Quartz, Black Onyx and Rock Crystal.

ADULTS ONLY - Rose Quartz, Amethyst and Carnelian.

TO REMOVE ACHES & PAINS: Rose Quartz, Hematite and Rock Crystal.

ELIXIR OF LIFE - Rhodonite and Sodalite.

ENERGY BOOSTER - Carnelian, Amethyst and Rock Crystal.

IMAGINE - Rose Quartz, Amethyst and Green Aventurine.

FERTILITY - Moonstone, Rose Quartz and Rock Crystal.

CONFIDENCE - Tiger Eye, Green Aventurine and Black Onyx.

Leeper's Ambiguous Lady or:-
"My Wife My Mother-in-Law' (first published November 6th 1915)

Can you see an attractive young lady or an old witch?
Objectively they are both present in the picture,
but it is impossible to see them both together.

See your local stockist for any Gemstones and Crystals mentioned in this publication. However, if you are having difficulty in obtaining any of the stones mentioned, we do offer our own mail order service and would be more than pleased to supply any of the stones listed.

If you like natural products, hand-crafted gifts
Including Gemstone jewellery, objects of natural beauty –
The finest examples from Mother Nature, tinged with
An air of Mystery – then we will not disappoint you.
For those who can enjoy that feeling of connection with the
Esoteric nature of Gemstones and Crystals, then our
'Power for Life' – Power Bracelets could be ideal for you.
Each bracelet comes with its own guide explaining a way of thinking that's
so powerful it will change your life and the information comes straight
from the Bible.

For further details - write to:
ROSEWOOD,
P.O. Box 219. Huddersfield, West Yorkshire. HD2 2YT

E-mail enquiries to: info@rosewood-gifts.co.uk

Or why not visit our website for even more information:
www.rosewood-gifts.co.uk

Gemstone and Crystal Birthstones
Astrology
the
Secret Code

"Discover your true birthstone
Your lucky Talisman"

By
Robert W. Wood D.Hp
(Diploma in Hypnotherapy)

Rosewood Publishing

BK8

It was the Greeks that gave us the now-familiar twelve signs of the Zodiac, but it was Carl Gustav Jung who, at the turn of the twentieth century, successfully linked his special form of Psychology with Astrology.

The 'Mean Average'.

Many years ago I became involved in a project to try to find a list of twelve genuine Birthstones. It was for a new business venture, selling birthstone gifts through party plan. However, when I started to research into many different sources, I quickly realised that they all seemed to be saying something different. No two seemed to say the same thing. I studied and researched over 17 different sources for information, including encyclopaedias, world famous psychics, mystics and astrologers.

I discovered that different continents favoured their own 'home-grown' gemstones and crystals, and that it was only a few hundred years ago that people first discovered how to cut a diamond (it takes a diamond to cut a diamond). Astrology is over six thousand years old, which means that a diamond couldn't have been an original birthstone. In the end, because of all these different lists, I decided the only way would be to take the mean average. That is: if the majority of my differing sources said Red Jasper was the birthstone for Aries then that was good enough for me; and so this was how I got my list - by using the mean average.

Discovering the 'true' Birthstones.

Imagine: I now had a list of twelve stones - but was it the right list? How could I find out? I asked well over two thousand people to help with my research, to see if I had got it right (if anyone can get it right!). To test my list I decided to put all the birthstones, in the form of tumblestones, into a basket. Then I passed the basket around, at the same time asking everyone if they would select a stone that they liked. I also asked them to tell me their star signs. Surprisingly, as it turned out, sometimes as many as 70% seemed to pick out their own stones, but a bigger surprise was that of those who didn't pick out their own birthstone, many picked out their 'opposite'. That means, for example, if they were Aries, then instead of picking out Red Jasper (their own birthstone) they picked out Green Aventurine, their 'opposite' stone (Libra). *More later.*

A secret code.

During my research I came across the 'Law of Polarity'. This states that everything has an opposite - for example: night and day, hot and cold, right and wrong, Ying and Yang etc. In astrology it means the opposite star sign becomes very important. That is, *the meaning of one is enhanced by the knowledge of the other*. If you do read your horoscopes, why not in future, for fun, read both your own and your opposite star sign. It may help you to gain a fuller picture. A list of 'opposites' starts on page 12.

I wondered - could there be another explanation why so many people, during my tests, seemed to be connected one way or another to their own or opposite birthstones? The answer, I think, may be: by colour. For example, on my list Aries' birthstone is Red Jasper. Surprisingly, over the years, I have often heard people say they don't like the colour of their own birthstone; and whenever I hear this I always suggest to them that they are more likely, if they are Aries, to like green - knowing that Green Aventurine (Libra) is their opposite star sign.

Gemstones and the Bible.

During my research, a friend told me that I could find the gemstones and crystals that I was researching in the Bible - but no-one at the time seemed to know exactly where. Then a very strange thing happened. It was a Thursday morning, I remember; I acquired a Bible, and looking at the last page I realised there were nearly 1,400 pages. I was just thinking how overwhelming all this would be - where do you start to look for Gemstone-Crystals? - when this strange 'something' happened.

I was thumbing my way through the Bible when a page seemed to open up. I was drawn to a story in Exodus. It's all about God asking Aaron, who will become the first High Priest, to fashion a 'Breastpiece'. And on this 'Breastpiece' God instructed him to place twelve stones, saying that these twelve stones would represent the twelve tribes of Israel.

I thought, 'This is symbolism.' In astrology, twelve stones represent the cycle of life and are called birthstones. However, within hours on the same day, I was drawn to another page. This was in the New Testament (Rev. 21-19) where it talks about a New Jerusalem; and there's another list of twelve stones. Now this list is different from the first, but this second list is very interesting because Red Jasper, which by using the mean average I had chosen to represent Aries in Astrology, was the first foundation for the New Jerusalem in the Scriptures.

So, being curious, I read on, only to find that the sixth foundation for the New Jerusalem was Carnelian - and Carnelian was the birthstone I had picked for Virgo, the sixth sign in Astrology. The twelfth foundation was Amethyst - and Amethyst was the same gemstone I had picked for Pisces, the twelfth sign.

The right Birthstones.

Is there a 'right' list of twelve stones? That's what I was trying to find. My list of twelve had come about after a great deal of extensive research, and included a lot of practical experience in front of thousands of people from all kinds of backgrounds, all walks of life. Well over 100,000 people have now heard my talk on the mysteries that surround gemstones and crystals, a talk entitled 'Discover the hidden powers of Gemstones'. I have read books containing named lists of precious stones, semi-precious stones, some have even suggested rough stones, and even stones that can represent the first half of a star sign with a totally different one representing the second half of the sign. Confusing, isn't it!

It's strange to think now, but by taking the mean average I have probably come closer than many in finding the right twelve, if it's possible to find the right twelve; unfortunately even the Scriptures don't help to resolve this dilemma by having two different lists.

A lucky Birthstone-Talisman.

During my product research I designed what's now turned out to be one of my most popular gifts. It's a special pair of eardrops: a classic line with the star sign gemstone at the base and the opposite star sign stone above, with

a spacer in between, on a sterling silver ear-wire. A talisman - a talisman is believed to protect the wearer from harm, and is thought to have magical powers. There's no stronger symbolism of the power of life than a birthstone, as it is a representation of our birth. Imagine all the power and energy that went into our arrival here on earth. So birthstones seem to act as lucky talismans. The secret here is that we may have more than one birthstone: our own, plus our opposite.

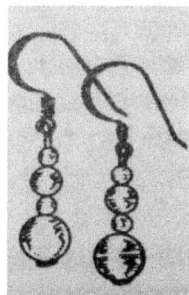

The 'law of polarity': the meaning of one is enhanced by the knowledge of the other. So don't forget in future, if you do read your horoscope, to read your opposite star sign. It will help you to gain a fuller picture.

Where did all this start?

According to the best scholars, Planet Earth started around 4,500 million years ago. Plants and insects such as beetles have been around for over 450 million years. Dinosaurs became extinct 65 million years ago. And, if you believe in evolution, man may have been around for 1 or even 2 million years. However, I find this curious: although some fossil evidence seems to exist, there seems to be no record of man's existence until about 28,000 years BC. Cave drawings have been found that have been dated to about this time. It's almost as if a few thousand years ago, man, as we know him today, just turned up - from where, we don't know.

Here's a thought: a scientist spent many months below ground, enjoying all his home comforts - except that he didn't know the time. Left to his own devices, he reverted to a 25-hour, not a 24-hour, day.

In prehistoric times, people were nomadic, always moving from one camp to another, until about 6,000 years ago when they began to settle down and build. They started to farm the land, keep animals and grow crops. The first civilisation, as we would know it, was probably at Sumer, which was situated in a broad, fertile valley between the rivers Tigris and Euphrates. This area was known then as Mesopotamia and is now known as Iraq.

The beginning of Astrology.

It is around this time that men started to record, through writings, their thoughts about minerals, precious stones, aromatherapy and star gazing; all, probably, with a view to improving their lives, their crops and their health, whilst at the same time seeking to protect themselves from their enemies, whether human, natural or even supernatural. They were seeking to see into the future, and generally trying to discover the many secrets of the world and universe.

The High Priests, the holy and learned men of their time, were carefully observing the night skies and plotting the course of the stars. They were also the ones performing religious rites, worshipping all the many pagan gods by asking for help. They performed all kinds of ceremonies and rituals. From this kind of science came Astrology. No-one knows where this information came from, only that it came.

These sages and High Priests seemed to know a lot about the 'Dog Star' Sirius, known as Sirius A, and its smaller companion star Sirius B - despite the fact that these two bodies are right outside our own solar system.

Sirius, the Dog Star, is the brightest star in the sky. The sages and High Priests thought that messengers from these systems had descended from the skies to earth to teach their ancestors good government and introduce them to a system for counting. This was at the time an intelligent interpretation of the facts then known.

Predicting the future.

Use your imagination - go back in time and imagine you have just arrived on the planet; it doesn't matter how, just that you have. You have no knowledge of Earth other than what you can see, touch, feel, taste and smell, but you do have one thing: your intelligence. You quickly realise that night follows day. After only a few years you will have noticed various seasons, each following on from the other; and so now you can see a pattern.

A logical start to this amazing 'pattern of life' would probably be soon after winter, around March or April, because then everything starts to grow. It then matures during summer, and bears fruit during autumn, before dying back in winter. Then this miracle of life starts all over again the following spring. So life is a cycle that repeats itself time after time after time. The Egyptian Priests took this knowledge and used it so accurately that they could foretell, each year, the flooding of the Nile to within a few days. Could this be the start of trying to see into the future?

The Birth of the Zodiac.

From 6,000 to 4,000 BC the Babylonians, Egyptians and Chinese all seem to have believed that the stars, representing the heavenly bodies, influenced the lives of all men. The Babylonians, in particular, thought that the positions of the stars represented messages from the gods, and their Priests spent much of their lives studying with great care. They divided the heavens into regions, and various groups of stars into constellations, naming each one after their many different pagan gods or objects.

Anybody who still thinks the sky is the limit
is short of imagination

Around 600 BC, the Greeks re-named these constellations and gave them the now-familiar Twelve Signs of the Zodiac.

As the earth rotated through the year's cycle, the positions of each constellation seemed to indicate when men should plant seeds or reap harvests, when to stock fuels for winter, and so from these simple observations the science of Astrology was born. The Greeks believed that humans, as well as gemstones and crystals, were all born under the influence of the planets. So a person born under the sign of Pisces, for example, would share their sign with the gemstone Amethyst. Therefore Amethyst is thought to be particularly beneficial and can act as a lucky talisman for those born under the star sign of Pisces. *More about birthstones later.*

Modern Astrology.

From the beginning of our history right up to the seventeenth century, an astrological view of things was the accepted norm. This influence can still be seen today in the architecture of many of our great churches and cathedrals. The Zodiac window at Chartres in France is a fine example of what is commonly known as a 'rose window', normally based on the number twelve or even sometimes twenty-four. It should not be forgotten that the founders of modern Astronomy, such as Johannes Kepler, Galileo Galilei and many others, were all court astrologers in their time.

Carl Gustav Jung (1875-1961).

Much of the work of Carl Gustav Jung, a Swiss psychotherapist, was concerned with the symbolism of dreams, myths and religions. Up until the publication of his work on the Psychology of the Unconscious in 1911, Carl Gustav Jung had been a leading collaborator with Sigmund Freud. Freud is the founder of modern-day psychology, and along with Carl Jung was mainly responsible for the 20th century's fascination with the subconscious. For reasons still unknown, the time of birth and the placements of the planets can tell a skilled astrologer a great deal about an individual's temperament, talents and even their hang-ups.

You can benefit hugely from this knowledge. Even the Church uses it. Astonishingly, they have discovered that it's possible to separate the physical from the spiritual. The Church knows this through the workings of 'Myers Briggs typology', developed by a mother-and-daughter team from America, who took the work of Carl Young and expanded on it. If you ever get the chance to go on a Myers-Briggs course, I can highly recommend it.

Psychological profiling and Astrology

Carl Jung's research into psychoanalysis led him into some fascinating interpretations of personality expressions which he called 'extraversion' and 'introversion' energy. It's surprising how closely these resemble the astrological understanding of positive and negative energy. See what you think when you read your own psychological profile later on.

If you can, imagine the twelve signs of the Zodiac as a symbolic representation of the various expressions of energy - as if the 'life force', symbolised by the planets, is diffused and refracted to express every kind of conceivable behavioural characteristic ever associated with man. The time of birth seems to dicate an individual's characteristics; so Astrology seems to have helped give birth to what we now know as psychological profiling.

Business and profiles.
Today, it's quite likely, if you apply for a position with any reasonable-sized company, that they will ask you not only to submit your current CV but also to fill out a psychological profile analysis sheet. This is to help them assess your suitability and your potential, the reason being that these 'profiles' are said to be well over 90% accurate. This is why companies are prepared to pay small fortunes to consultants to help them to recruit only the very best. And how do they find the best? They ask questions.

They will ask questions without you knowing the reason behind the question. For example: Which word in each pair appeals to you more?
Gentle or Firm   Soft or Hard   Speak or Write   Sign or Symbol

Or: At parties, do you
(A) sometimes get bored, or (B) always have fun?

Or: Would you rather work under someone who is
(A) always kind, or (B) always fair?

There are no 'right' or 'wrong' answers to the above questions. Your answers will help show how you look at things, and how you like to make decisions. If, from this, they decide you're not suitable, you won't even be given the chance of an interview. This is 'mind-blowing' stuff: do they really know that much about us? The answer, surprisingly, is: Yes, they do. Remember - they are said to be well over 90% accurate. However, turn this around, and if you are offered an interview after you have taken a psychological profile, then I would ask for more money, because you've already passed their test.

Michael Gauquelin (1928-1991).

Although a psychologist, he was also an exponent of modern statistical method. He was the first scientist to demonstrate a firm connection between the state of the Solar system, the time of birth and success in certain professions, and between specific planets and character traits. Yes, finally science does seem to be catching up. Gauquelin's findings centre exclusively upon the planets. He worked mostly in his native country France, mainly because every French citizen since the Revolution (1792) has had the exact time of birth recorded on their birth certificate, as well as the date and place.

Scientific experiment.

His first experiment was back in 1951, when he studied the birth details of well over five hundred members of the French Academy of Medicine. You would of course expect their times of birth to be random. However, that's not what he seems to have found. Way beyond any statistical coincidence, he discovered a strong connection with Mars and Saturn. At first, being quite sceptical, Gauquelin checked his results against a control group of people taken randomly from the register of births, and spread throughout the day. Their birth times made no planetary pattern whatsoever

By way of a double check, he looked at another five hundred plus doctors and came up with the same distinct Mars and Saturn connection, just as he had with the members of the Academy of Medicine. For most of his life, Gauquelin rejected traditional astrology, insisting instead that his research pointed to an entirely new pathway in science. Sadly, both then and now he's been thought of as an outcast, a heretic in the eyes of the scientific establishment.

Some amazing findings.

If he did appear to be onto something with his findings about eminent doctors, his subsequent discoveries suggest that this 'something' is pretty big. He researched notable writers, playwrights and journalists and found that they tended to have a connection with the Moon. Looking at actors, top executives and politicians he discovered that many more than average were born with a strong connection with Jupiter. His strongest findings of all, double the significant incidence of any other results, was the regularity with which Mars appeared in the natal charts of top-class athletes. If the pace of change continues then astrology will gain a more respectable, credible image as the twenty-first century progresses.

A sales manager's findings.

A sales manager quickly realised that over 75% of all his sales were being brought in by just three of the star signs: Aries, Gemini and Aquarius; and so he only hired people born under these star signs. It may not be as daft as it sounds, because all three signs are fast-moving and fast-thinking. Aries can be pushy and very competitive. Gemini and Aquarians are word spinners.

The Law of Polarity.

On the following pages I have outlined each sign of the Zodiac and conveniently placed on the same page its opposite star sign. If you imagine your own star sign as representing you - the 'you' others can see - then your opposite is representative of your inner world, a world others can't see. A world from within; your inner thoughts; a world only you can visit. Also, you will find your birthstones. If you find you are being drawn more to your opposite birthstone, you now have within this book an explanation of why. The combination of the two can, I believe, create a very powerful lucky talisman. It's the secret code, the Law of Polarity.

Negative traits

And finally, a word about the negative traits. So often I've heard people say that they don't like them or that these traits are nothing like them. Let me say, it's rare that you will see the negative traits in anybody unless life is really being cruel, or they are ill. Look upon them as God's gifts to survive; there are circumstances in everybody's life when these traits can become very valuable. Think about this: sometimes we need to be *manipulative, impatient, obsessive, restless, uncompromising, detached, dictatorial, materialistic* or *rebellious*. You may agree with me that without all these 'negative' traits Bob Geldoff would never have been able to create Band Aid, one of the most successful charity events of modern times.

For further details - write to: ROSEWOOD,
P.O. Box 219, Huddersfield, West Yorkshire. HD2 2YT
E-mail enquiries to: info@rosewood-gifts.co.uk
www.rosewood-gifts.co.u

Aries - opposite star sign - **Libra**

Aries 21st March - 20th April   Birthstone - Red Jasper
The Ram   The First House (ruled by Mars)
                    Key Phrase - 'I have to know who I am'

Ariens have a straightforward and positive attitude to life. They need adventure and like to take risks. They are passionate and sexy people but can be aggressive and dominating. They are optimistic; they believe in and create their own luck, tackling life in an uncomplicated fashion. They are viewed as enterprising self-starters, naturally more impulsive, buoyant, communicative and sociable. Associated with the high-octane energy and enthusiasm of youth.

Positive traits - courageous, enthusiastic, independent, forthright. Negative traits - extravagant, impulsive, brash, selfish, impatient.
Element Fire
'Let's get on with it, now I am here'

*[Now read your opposite sign **Libra** for a fuller picture]*

Libra - opposite star sign - **Aries**

Libra 23rd Sept - 23rd Oct   Birthstone - Green Aventurine
The Scales   The Seventh House (ruled by Venus)
                    Key Phrase - 'I must justify my existence'

This is the sign of fair play and harmony. Librans are charmers who enjoy socialising and do not like to feel left out. They manage to appear calm in situations but can be indecisive. They are concerned with the realms of ideas. Libra symbolises the winds of change that bring fresh opportunities for growth, creative thought, exchanging and spreading information. They like the challenge of finding the balance between the needs of others and personal desire.

Positive traits - gracious, cheerful, charming, refined and diplomatic. Negative traits - manipulative, procrastinating and indecisive.
Element Air
'What is going on and why, I have to know?'

*[Now read your opposite sign **Aries** for a fuller picture]*

Taurus - opposite star sign - **Scorpio**

Taurus 21st April - 21st May   **Birthstone - Rose Quartz**
The Bull   The Second House (ruled by Venus)
                   Key Phrase - 'I need to see what I am'

Taureans are very loyal, sensible and reliable but need security and routine in their lives. They are passionate lovers but can be very possessive and sometimes stubborn. They are down-to-earth yet can be forceful. Their reliability in being constantly productive and precise leads them to top positions. Their creative and imaginative nature provides the ability to succeed in their chosen career. They can focus on using available resources to achieve practical ends.

Positive traits - sincere, reliable, faithful, solid and dependable.
Negative traits - obsessive, possessive, naive, obstinate and plodding.
Element Earth
'I don't yet know what it's all about, so I'll wait'

*[Now read your opposite sign **Scorpio** for a fuller picture]*

Scorpio - opposite star sign - **Taurus**

Scorpio 24th Oct - 22nd Nov   **Birthstone - Rhodonite**
The Scorpion   The Eighth House (ruled by Mars & Pluto)
                   Key Phrase - 'I am not alone'

Scorpios are energetic, intense, sensual people and concern themselves with deep hidden meanings, constantly seeking what lies beneath the surface. They have the ability to 'read between the lines'. They enjoy positions of power and tend to be strong-willed. They are secretive and jealous, can be possessive with partners, and enjoy active sexual relationships. They are protective, nurturing and compassionate.

Positive traits - resourceful, decisive, penetrating and focused.
Negative traits - resentful, vindictive, sarcastic, jealous and cunning.
Element Water
'To see if my first impressions are correct, I shall wait'

*[Now read your opposite sign **Taurus** for a fuller picture]*

133

Gemini - opposite star sign - **Sagittarius**

Gemini 22nd May - 21st June   **Birthstone - Black Onyx**
The Twins   The Third House (ruled by Mercury)
Key Phrase - 'I need to know why I am'

Very chatty, lively people who have a quick, light-hearted wit. They make good salespeople with their natural ability to sell and get on with people. Geminis can be charming, versatile and very often have the capacity to be bi-lingual. These excellent communicators have the ability to relate fascinating stories when speaking in public, although they can be impatient with others. At their best, their active, analytical mind can make sense of the relationship between things.

Positive traits - humorous, communicative, versatile and spontaneous. Negative traits - restless, fickle, detached and inclined to exaggerate.
Element Air
'What is going on and why, I have to know'

*[Now read your opposite sign **Sagittarius** for a fuller picture]*

Sagittarius - opposite star sign - **Gemini**

Sagittarius 23rd Nov - 21st Dec   **Birthstone - Sodalite**
The Centaur   The Ninth House (ruled by Jupiter)
Key Phrase - 'I love to live'

These are the hunters who need freedom and stimulation. Sagittarians are enthusiastic and fun-loving, and have a thirst for knowledge. They are optimists, always open to new experiences, and love adventure and travel. They need a lot of understanding, as they can be unreliable and restless, especially within the confines of a relationship. They do, however, usually achieve emotional happiness and material success. Their luck sees them through.

Positive traits - frank, logical, kind, generous, optimistic and honest. Negative traits - extravagant, quarrelsome, blunt and dictatorial.
Element Fire
'Let's get on with it, now I am here'

*[Now read your opposite sign **Gemini** for a fuller picture]*

Cancer - opposite star sign - Capricorn

Cancer 22nd June - 22nd July   **Birthstone - Mother of Pearl**
The Crab   The Fourth House (ruled by the Moon)
                Key Phrase - 'I must know my origins'

Cancerians are very nice, charming, caring and sensitive people. However, they do have a tendency to worry, although more often they are self-assured and resourceful. They also tend to be extremely sensitive to the moods and emotional undercurrents around them. They are very faithful, making very good long-term friends. They are receptive to the needs of partners and those close to them. They can comprehend that which is not necessarily seen; they have great insight.

Positive traits - industrious, thrifty, loyal, sympathetic and sensitive. Negative traits - secretive, capricious, cloying, touchy and clingy.
Element Water
'To see if my first impressions are correct, I shall wait'

*[Now read your opposite sign **Capricorn** for a fuller picture]*

Capricorn - opposite star sign - Cancer

Capricorn 22nd Dec- 20th Jan   **Birthstone - Obsidian Snowflake**
The Goat   The Tenth House (ruled by Saturn)
                Key Phrase - 'Nil Desperandum' ('Never give up')

Capricorns are ambitious, hardworking, independent individuals, empire-builders who enjoy good taste and achieve success later in life. They have a tendency to be bossy when pursuing prestige and power. They can be stubborn in their need for financial security and stability. However, they have good organising skills and are cautious and realistic, with high standards. They are scrupulous, fearless and sure-footed, traits that lead to becoming self-made, successful people.

Positive traits - profound, efficient, ambitious and hard working. Negative traits - gloomy, materialistic, arrogant and intolerant.
Element Earth
'I don't yet know what it's all about, so I'll wait'

*[Now read your opposite sign **Cancer** for a fuller picture]*

135

Leo - opposite star sign - **Aquarius**

Leo 23rd July - 23rd Aug   **Birthstone - Tiger Eye**
The Lion   The Fifth House (ruled by the Sun)
                Key Phrase - 'I am capable of becoming more'

Leos are born leaders and organisers who are creative and charismatic. They always enjoy life to the full. They are generous and like spending money. They are warm and enthusiastic. Although they can be dominating and vain, Leos tend to make it to the top. They are creative, honest and loyal, courageous to the point of self-sacrifice, with a pride in their work and their home. They show great strength when under a lot of pressure or when in a crisis. Leos have a sunny disposition.

Positive traits - hospitable, affectionate, regal and magnanimous. Negative traits - self-centred, uncompromising, vain and domineering.

Element Fire
'Let's get on with it, now I am here'

*[Now read your opposite sign **Aquarius** for a fuller picture]*

Aquarius - opposite star sign - **Leo**

Aquarius 21st Jan - 19th Feb   **Birthstone - Blue Agate**
The Water Carrier   The Eleventh House (ruled by Saturn & Uranus)
                Key Phrase - 'I belong to the family of man'

Aquarians make excellent friends; they are understanding and faithful. They are complex characters, original, magnetic, inventive and visionary. They are witty, chatty and sharp with independent minds. They can appear eccentric at times. They are communicative, thoughtful, caring and scientific, hence their complex characters. Aquarian ideas may be unusual and original, but once formed they tend to remain fixed and focused, which shows their independence of thought and action.

Positive traits - trustworthy, caring, friendly and broad-minded.
Negative traits - unpredictable, moody, rebellious and impersonal.

Element Air
'What is going on and why, I have to know'

*[Now read your opposite sign **Leo** for a fuller picture]*

136

Virgo - opposite star sign - **Pisces**

Virgo 24th Aug - 22nd Sept   **Birthstone - Carnelian**
The Virgin The Sixth House (ruled by Mercury)
     Key Phrase - 'I must always strive for perfection'

Virgos are workers, practical and neat in every way. They can be perfectionists and are capable of giving self-sacrificing service to others, although they may be critical of them. They are very genuine, powerful people but they tend to worry, although they are the ones who can improve stability and create order from apparent chaos. Virgos almost crave the opportunity to serve others and take charge. They have a gentleness with the helpless, and are sympathetic and well-organised.

Positive traits - painstaking, analytical, studious and considerate. Negative traits - detached, sceptical, prone to worry, and cynical.
Element Earth
'I don't yet know what it's all about, so I'll wait'

*[Now read your opposite sign **Pisces** for a fuller picture]*

Pisces – opposite star sign - **Virgo**

Pisces 20th Feb - 20th March   **Birthstone - Amethyst**
The Fish The Twelfth House (ruled by Jupiter & Neptune)
     Key Phrase - 'I wish I could come back some other time'

Pisceans are the dreamers, creative and imaginative, but lacking confidence. They are very loving, caring, sensitive and kind; they are lovers of peace. They may lack ambition, can be vague and indecisive, and sometimes lack the insight for promotion through their inability to promote themselves. They like discipline and are ideal for tasks where regular duties are called for. They are trusting, hospitable and will help anyone in distress. Pisces is a sign of a 'healer'.

Positive traits - unassuming, courteous, imaginative, gentle and lenient. Negative traits - apologetic, changeable and self-pitying.
Element Water
'To see if my first impressions are correct, I shall wait'

*[Now read your opposite sign **Virgo** for a fuller picture]*

Lucky Gemstone and Crystal

Talismans
Charms
and
Amulets

For
Health, Wealth and Happiness

By
Robert W. Wood D.Hp
(Diploma in Hypnotherapy)

Rosewood Publishing

BK9

TALISMANS, CHARMS AND AMULETS

In our world of scientific achievements,
with its computers, aeroplanes, rockets, space travel
and the Internet, isn't it surprising to find that there still
remains an ancient 'magical-like' knowledge that
retains its grip on the human imagination.
And it's found in the form of lucky
Talismans, Charms and Amulets.

Talismans.

A talisman is often a stone or other small object, sometimes inscribed or carved on, and believed to protect the wearer from evil influences, bad luck, mischief or ill health. The word 'talisman' comes from the Greek word 'telesma' meaning 'to consecrate or magically charge'. Throughout history, magical talismans have been used to help bring protection, power and prosperity to their wearer or owner. They are specifically designed to achieve a particular purpose, and are said to work by generating a positive energy that can help to achieve this.

Amulets.

Unlike talismans that need to be 'charged', amulets come already imbued with their own built-in power for health, wealth, energy, good luck and so on. There is a certain passiveness associated with the powers of an amulet. The possessor only needs to 'connect' by carrying, wearing or being near to it. The word 'amulet' is probably derived from the Latin 'amuletum', and may also have come from an Arab term 'hamala', which means 'to carry'.

Charms.

A charm is often a small object, a trinket, a piece of jewellery, and is often worn on a bracelet - a 'charm bracelet' - to protect, influence or heal, to attract good luck etc; a 'lucky charm'. The name is connected to the uttering of magical chants, a condition of 'enchantment'. The word 'charm' comes from the Latin word 'carmen' meaning 'a song'.

Using a kind of magic, a talisman can be endowed with a kind of supernatural power. This can be done either by using the forces of nature (for example, putting the talisman into a stream), or by a divine power (saying prayers), or by a ritualistic ceremony; or even by a combination of all three, depending on who's doing the 'charging'.

The word 'magic' can be used in many different ways. I use the word often in the sense that a spectacular fireworks display could be described as 'magical'. We live on a 'magical' planet; who could fail to be impressed by the splendour of a clear night sky, a sunrise or sunset, an electrical storm, a snowflake, spring flowers or autumn leaves? Or we can use the word 'magic' to mean any mysterious or extraordinary quality or power; you, the reader, will have to decide what is meant when you read 'magic' or 'magical'.

Throughout the ages.

A talisman can be any object that's believed to be endowed with magical powers. The item is active when it bestows this magical power upon the one who possesses it. Remember the story of Jack and the Beanstalk; it was the beans that were magical - they had been supercharged to grow into something very special: a giant beanstalk.

The Egyptians and Babylonians used talismans when attempting to alter the forces of nature. In the Middle Ages, holy relics and other objects assumed the value of talismans in attempts to cure illnesses.

There is a long tradition throughout history of talismans being made by alchemists, shamans, witches and priests. Alchemical charms were often worn by Kings and Queens, diplomats and merchants, popes and bishops. Less expensive amulets, usually made by witches, were worn or hung in the house by nearly everybody else. The most common amulets were those that protected against violence, plague, theft and bad luck.

Many alchemists sought the assistance of talismans, which they made in elaborate ceremonies. These were conducted during periods of auspicious astrological occasions, an example being during a full moon. Whilst performing these rituals they would recite incantations to conjure up the desired spirits, the ones who would imbue the talisman with magical power.

A talisman most sought after would have been the 'Philosopher's Stone', which many alchemists thought would transform base metals into silver or gold, therefore transforming, at the same time, their own fortunes.

J. K. Rowling, author of the book 'Harry Potter and the Philosopher's Stone', which has also been made into a film, changed it and decided that the Philosopher's Stone, for her, would be the 'Elixir of Life'.

Some legendary lucky talismans.

Who could forget that the sword 'Excalibur' gave King Arthur magical powers? Followers of St. Patrick, the patron saint of Ireland, have adopted the Shamrock as a symbol of luck - 'the luck of the Irish'. During the time of the Crusades, Nordic countries employed their special magical alphabet known as the 'Runes' for protection.

Legend has it that the undead (vampires) cannot attack if you hold up a cross - the symbol of God - as good deflects evil. Although crosses are not employed as a deflector of vampires today, at most Catholic funerals many attendees have crucifixes around their necks, although they probably don't usually wear them as everyday jewellery. The Christian fish, an ancient sign of Christ, is often seen on the backs of cars as an amulet, signifying that the owner wishes to be protected from evil. The scarab, the sacred beetle of ancient Egypt, is thought to possess the power to control the Sun and Immortality.

The lists goes on and on. Here are a few more: a horseshoe, a corn dolly, a dream-catcher, the seal of Solomon, the Kara, the ankh, a Buddha, the crescent, a St. Christopher, a lucky elephant, owl, cat or frog, a four-leafed clover, a wishbone, a wheel and so many more, depending on your culture.

Just like amulets, talismans play a significant part in everyday life. For example, in most religious traditions sacred books like the Torah, the Bible and the Koran are believed by some to possess special protective powers. This power is even carried over into the law courts of the world, where we swear to tell the truth by placing our hand on a holy book.

Modern talismans

Think of a rosary. Although the precise number of beads may vary from religion to religion, the purpose remains the same: to keep count of the number of devotional prayers being recited. But some believe they also have special protective powers.

New knowledge.

Although science has now an explanation for many of the phenomena that once baffled us, it is still a long way from being able to explain all of the mysteries that surround life. This is often left to others, and this is where religion or philosophy seems to step in and try to help. In ancient times it would have been alchemists, shamans, witches and priests. A few decades ago, computers, telephones, rockets, planes and satellites would have been objects described by everyone as being 'magical' or fanciful.

New knowledge seems to be arriving on a daily basis and at breakneck, phenomenal speed. Have you noticed how time seems to be speeding up? We have now truly entered into a new world, and this world is based on an incredible amount of knowledge.

It now begs the question: can talismans, charms and amulets have a place in this new world?

You may be surprised, but I think the answer is still 'yes', because I believe they fulfil an important role. They form a bridge from the past to the future, because they still can excite the imagination. Understand: I don't think they are a substitute for our natural instincts or built-in 'inner powers' or wisdom; but they can be a useful tool to help us see and then use the 'universal life force' that is inherent throughout the whole of the universe and in the forces of nature.

With the help of our minds, and especially our imaginations, and by employing our knowledge, we can begin to use this 'magic' to enrich both our own and others' lives. We are beginning to see that nature, the 'universal life force', mysteriously is interlinked with our bodies, minds and spirits.

Discovering a greater meaning.

The function of a talisman is to help make things possible; to bring about powerful transformations; to help a person who would not feel confident within themselves without a little help. A talisman can initially be that help. It's a useful tool. It's a little like phoning a helpline - you have a problem and you need help - except there's no-one there to take your call, only an answering machine. So you leave a message and hope someone will listen and then get back to you with help later. In this analogy the phone represents the talisman; it's the tool, it's a way of connecting.

Our journey through life is all about personal empowerment and freedom of choice, and what we do with it. Some people seem to be able to manifest their own power quite naturally, whilst others struggle to get past anything that controls their 'free will'. And so throughout the history of humanity, people have placed their hope in inanimate objects, in the belief of gaining that extra little help.

Be lucky.

Whether you are a believer in the supernatural or not, to have a sense of control over the uncontrollable is one explanation for why many seem to believe in lucky talismans. This belief crosses all nationalities, intelligence, education and status.

I remember reading about a chairman of an amazingly successful company which was growing at a very rapid rate. A reporter who asked him if he could explain the reason behind his company's rapid growth may have been forgiven for being a little surprised at the answer: the chairman quite flippantly explained it was all down to his magic lucky beans, and then showed him some he had on his desk in the form of sweets.

Don't we all, in one way or another, practise rituals to attract good luck? Take a bride, for example: to attract good luck she will wear something old, something new, something borrowed and something blue. On the first day of each new month some people will say 'rabbits, rabbits' for good luck. How many people won't walk under ladders, or, if they spill salt, throw some over their left shoulder so as to avoid attracting bad luck.

Some will turn over their money in their pockets at the sight of a new moon in the hope of attracting more. How about: 'If you see a penny, pick it up, and all the day you'll have good luck'.

Luck may be an illusion of control, but control is what we seek in a random world. Although it may have no basis in science, it certainly can affect how we feel. Talismans, lucky charms and amulets can give a sense of preparedness, a feeling of control and a more positive outlook on life, which in itself may give us that edge to help improve our lives for the better. We all need something to believe in, be it a faith, a lucky mascot, a talisman or a philosophy. You may be surprised to find what even Prime Ministers' wives believe in.

The Bioelectrical Shield.

In 1998 the British Prime Minister's wife, Cherie Blair, was seen wearing a 'stress-busting' metal-encased crystal talisman, a pendant said to contain a 'magical' configuration of quartz and other crystals which help to deflect away from the wearer negative electromagnetic radiation, the kind that's emitted from modern office equipment such as computers and mobile phones.

Designed by a chiropractor called Dr. Charles Brown in the early 1990s, the shield has proved immensely popular despite its high selling price. The formula for the pendant and the crystal configuration came to the doctor in a series of visions, when he heard voices telling him what to do.

Cherie Blair was reported to have said, after she had misplaced her shield once, how she had become distressed because, as she explained it, 'It keeps away the bad vibrations from my computer.' This must be the very latest, certainly the most modern of all talismans. Since time began men or women have found comfort in the belief that they are not alone; that there's more to life than meets the eye. This is what all the great religions, philosophers, teachers, mystics, holy men, sages and priests have all been saying; maybe one day, somehow, we will discover they were all telling the truth.

George Frederick Kunz (1856-1932).

Some of the oldest ever recorded talismans appear in a brilliant book called 'The Magic of Jewels & Charms', written by George Frederick Kunz in 1915. He was a distinguished self-taught mineralogist who, for more than half a century, was the gem expert for Tiffany & Co. New York. Here are a few extracts taken from his original book of 1915.

... among the many stones endowed by medieval belief with wonderful powers, may be reckoned the 'rainmaking stones'. The miraculous effect was produced by rubbing them against each other ...

... Oriental rain-stones noted by ... writers of medieval times ... rock crystal as a rain-compeller finds honour among the wizards of the Ta-Ta-Thi tribe in New South Wales, Australia ...

... A mysterious stone mentioned three times in the Old Testament, each signifies a material noted for its hardness and translated 'diamond';

144

however, as it is almost certain that the Hebrews were not familiar with the 'diamond' it was most probably a variety of corundum ...

... fabled gem-bearing dragons of India were said to have sometimes fallen victims to the enchanter's art ...

... a stone described by Thomas de Cantimpre ... taken from the heart of a man poisoned, and kept for nine years, it gave protection from lightning, sudden death ...

... St. Hildegard of Bingen (1098 - 1179) wrote that 'just as a poisonous herb placed on a man's skin will produce ulceration'; by an analogous though contrary effect certain precious stones will, if placed on the skin, confer health and sanity by their virtue ...

How did she know? She heard voices telling her, in visions. She was one of the outstanding females of the 12th century and probably of the entire Middle Ages. She was a painter, composer, poet, scientist, playwright, prophet, preacher, abbess - and healer. From the time she was a young girl, Hildegard experienced visions. She claimed that angels described to her the healing properties of at least 25 stones.

... for centuries or more countless thousands, feeling assured of spiritual immortality, were nonetheless eager to have eternal youth and vigour and the power to peer into the future ...

Alchemists
... desire to find something by means of which gold could be made out of base metals; for youth and vigour, if coupled with poverty, are only half blessings. The search for the 'philosopher's stone' ... aimless pursuits of this end .. helped to lay the foundation of our modern chemistry...

... whether the conscious aim of the alchemist was the discovery of an actual stone, or merely the discovery of some process for turning a valueless substance into one of great value, is not clearly ascertainable from the purposely vague and obscure treatise on alchemy (Kunz is referring here to Ponce de Leon's 'Quest for the Foundation of Youth')

... the Alchemists believed that several other stones possessing 'magical' virtues could be produced. Among them: the Angelic stone, which gave power to see the angels in dreams and visions, and also the 'mineral stone', a substance by means of which common flints could be transmuted into diamonds, rubies, sapphires, emeralds etc.

Possibly some alchemists were glassmakers and fused the quartz with various mineral salts into an imitation of the gems, therefore having the colours but not the hardness or other properties.

Stones.
... in British New Guinea - a native, who was suffering from Lumbago, fully believed the tale that his disease was caused by a stone embedded in his flesh. When the 'sorcerer' made passes over this man's back and pretended to remove a stone, the sufferer was convinced that the disease had left his body and he began to feel relief ...

...the burying of white stones or lumps of quartz with the dead was not infrequent in early times, in Ireland ... symbolic meaning of the colour of purity, white marble seems appropriate and beautiful for monuments ....

St. Columba went to the river Ness and picked up out of its shallows several white pebbles - announcing that they would, by the Lord's power, work the cure of 'heathen' people. One of the stones was blessed by the saint and placed in a vessel filled with water; having taken a drink, the liquid restored his health ...

... a famous Scotch amulet - white quartz owned by the chiefs of Clan Donnachaidh and known as the 'stone of the Banner' ... was looked upon when first found as a powerful talisman in battle. And water in which it had been dipped was said to cure disease...

... the influence exercised by the text in Revelation (2.17): 'to him that overcometh ... I will give a white stone, and in the stone a new name written, which no man knoweth save he that receiveth it'.

... collections of stones and pebbles, often of little or no intrinsic value but supposed to possess occult powers, are handed down from father to son in many Hindu families of the poorer class ...

Amber.
... in ancient and medieval times the fear of poison being administered in food or drink was very great; and any substance that was credited with the power to show the presence of poison, by

146

some change in clearness or colour, was highly valued. An Amber cup was said to reveal various kinds of poison ...

... the electrical property of amber was remarked as early as 600 B.C. by the Ionic philosopher Thales, and from this observation may be dated the beginning of the study of electrical phenomena ...

Romans used to hold balls of amber in their hands to keep cool ... the Chinese place pieces of amber on or in their pillows ... as proof of the extravagant value set upon amber by the Romans, sold at a higher figure than did a healthy, vigorous slave ...

Loadstone.

...in the seventeenth century a rupture, it was reported, was cured in 8 days by loadstone. The patient was first given a dose of iron filings, reduced to a very fine powder. A plaster made from crushed loadstone was applied externally to the affected part...

... in Medieval Europe, this mineral (loadstone) was greatly valued for its therapeutic virtues. Trotula, the first of the female physicians connected with the celebrated school of Salerno, the centre of medical culture in Europe in the Middle Ages ... recommended the use of loadstone in childbirth. The stone was to be held in the right hand ...

... That wounds caused by burning could be healed if powdered loadstone were sprinkled over them, was confidently taught even in the seventeenth century ...

A magnetised piece of steel looks exactly the same as an ordinary piece of steel - but the magnetised one can lift over twelve times its own weight, whereas the ordinary steel could not even lift a feather.

Magical protection.

There's always been a fascinating history or a symbolic background to talismans, charms and amulets. Even people who do not subscribe to the idea of magical protection will usually have some little object that they keep about them 'just for luck'; a little something just to help when facing the hazards of daily life.

Among these talismans and amulets are often found precious and semi-precious gemstones and crystals, each one possessing its own 'magical', historical and evolutionary curative power, a gift from nature; but can any be more beautiful than 'Birthstones' - steeped in history, born at the very beginning of the birth of our knowledge.

Birthstones.
Birthstones are used as lucky talismans to help bring good luck, health, wealth and happiness, and are often given to a new-born child. I have realised, mainly because of the many talks I have given over the years on 'the mysteries that surround gemstones and crystals', that most people seem to 'know' which their birthstone is; for example, it may be a diamond or a sapphire, an emerald or a ruby, a garnet or an opal, an amethyst or a pearl, etc, etc. They think, therefore, that the following list must be wrong. However, I discovered there are many lists. My list, printed below, contains only semi-precious gemstones. (To learn how I acquired this list, you'll find out more in my book 'Discover Why Crystal Healing Works'; details from the publishers - their address is given on the last page.)

However, I would like you to think about this: a diamond could not have been one of the original birthstones, because astrology dates back easily over six thousand years and no-one knew how to cut a diamond then. The art of cutting a diamond was only discovered a few hundred years ago, mainly because it takes a diamond to cut a diamond. So the diamond could not have been among the birthstones at that time. It now seems probable that what people mistook for a diamond was more likely to have been rock crystal.

After thorough and exhaustive research, I believe I have been able to establish as near genuine a list of birthstones as it is possible to get. My research was helped a lot, surprisingly, from the Scriptures, where there are two lists of twelve stones, one in the New and one in the Old Testament.

Sign	Dates		Birthstone
Aries	21st Mar -	20th April	Red Jasper
Taurus....................	21st April -	21st May	Rose Quartz
Gemini...................	22nd May -	21st June	Black Onyx
Cancer...................	22nd June -	22nd July	Mother of Pearl
Leo.........................	23rd July -	23rd Aug	Tiger Eye
Virgo.....................	24th Aug -	22nd Sept	Carnelian
Libra	23rd Sept -	23rd Oct	Green Aventurine
Scorpio	24th Oct -	22nd Nov	Rhodonite
Sagittarius..............	23rd Nov -	21st Dec	Sodalite
Capricorn...............	22nd Dec -	20th Jan.	Obsidian Snowflake
Aquarius	21st Jan -	19th Feb	Blue Agate
Pisces....................	20th Feb -	20th Mar	Amethyst

Theme stones.

The following lucky talismans and amulets are a list of stones taken from our range that's collectively been called 'Theme Stones. It's a range of the unusual and the humorous. There's a 'theme' behind each one, and although seemingly humorous at times, nevertheless they have been extensively researched to help find the right Gemstone or Crystal to create the ideal match for the following list of popular titles.

A Lucky *'Bingo Stone'*   **Obsidian Snowflake**
Carry this Gemstone with you and it may well be the way to your 'Jackpot'.

A *'Good Luck Stone'*   **Indian - Moonstone**
Allow this special Lucky Gemstone to help you attract your heart's desires.

'Lose a Stone' (for the weight watcher)   **Black Onyx**
Let this stone be your constant reminder to resist temptation.

'Love Stones'   **Amethyst**
Recognised as the Gemstone of true love, romance and faithfulness.

A *'Lucky Lottery Stone'*   **Green Aventurine**
Let the magical powers of this Gemstone help pick your winning numbers.

'Memory Stone' (to remember all)   **Rhodonite**
Memory going? Keep forgetting things? Then try this amazing Gemstone.

Achieve with a *'Milestone'*   **Red Jasper**
Aim for the top - set your targets and use this stone to achieve.

'Tranquillity Stone' for relaxing   **Rock Crystal**
Find your inner peace and calmness. and relax away your worries.

Use a *'Worry Stone'* to forget   **Tiger Eye**
Forget your problems. ease your mind. lift your spirits. and feel free.

For passion, an *'Adults Only Stone'*   **Carnelian**
A sensuous. imaginative aphrodisiac for those special 'adult' occasions.
(There should be a health warning with this stone, Wow)

Please Note
Any information given in this book is not intended to be taken
as a replacement for medical advice. Any person with a condition
requiring medical attention should consult a qualified doctor or therapist.
On no account should a gemstone or crystal ever be swallowed.

Power Gems.
Gemstones and crystals are used as lucky talismans and amulets. There are times when they are better known for their healing powers. I have been extensively researching the healing nature of stones for many years. I have looked at many different sources for my information, including the Scriptures, always trying to discover the true identity of the most powerful and popular healing stones. Many are renowned for their mysterious, often 'magical-like' hidden powers. For thousands of years, ancient civilisations have been using these stones to help heal the mind. body and spirit. They were used to help attract to their owners their share of good luck. health. wealth and energy.

Although stones and crystals are very much a part of nature, these lovely, shiny. colourful stones and crystals are likened to a 'magnetic field'. They influence those coming into contact with them. You cannot see microwaves or radio waves but you know they exist. Each crystal, having its own unique 'signature' in the form of its 'energy frequency' , allows us to tune into that same frequency like changing the station on a television set. In this case you tune in to the 'healing' channel.

A Guide to the Power Within.
The following unique groups of Gemstones and Crystals are designed to carefully link in harmony and unite their individual mystic powers to

provide a holistic 'force of energy', which can help revive health, increase wealth, bring peace and provide energy and vitality.

Healer.
Here are the three most powerful healing gemstones and crystals found during our research ..**Carnelian, Red Jasper and Rock Crystal.**

Good Luck.
The luckiest three Gemstones, all having a strong history with being lucky .... **Obsidian Snowflake, Green Aventurine and Moonstone.**

Peace of Mind.
A combination of stones to help bring peace, harmony and tranquillity into our surroundings**Green Aventurine, Rose Quartz and Rhodonite.**

For Willpower.
Stones and crystals that help to boost willpower, for losing weight or stopping smoking...........**Rose Quartz, Black Onyx and Rock Crystal.**

Adults Only.
Combining stones to create the most imaginative aphrodisiac; a very sensuous combination ....**Amethyst, Rose Quartz and Carnelian.**

To Remove Aches and Pains.
When combined together, this combination can work wonders on aches and pains.................**Hematite, Rock Crystal and Rose Quartz.**

To Lift Depression.
A combination of stones that can help bring back joy and happiness whilst removing sadness..............**Carnelian, Tiger Eye and Hematite.**

The Elixir of Life.
To produce this: wash the stones, place in a glass of water, leave overnight, and sip slowly. Produces youthfulness**Rhodonite and Sodalite.**

Energy Booster.
Designed to help with tiredness; helps to see and feel 'life' with more energy, vigour and vitality.....**Carnelian, Amethyst and Rock Crystal.**

Imagine.
Designed for a very special purpose, this helps to reach a level 'within the mind' for change......**Green Aventurine, Amethyst and Rose Quartz.**

Fertility.
Crystal power designed to increase fertility, for that extra little help just when it's needed.......**Rock Crystal, Rose Quartz and Moonstone.**

Wisdom.
Gain the ability to think and act wisely using knowledge, insight, understanding and experience....**Amethyst, Rose Quartz & Rock Crystal.**

The Modus Operandi.
Whether you can believe in these mystical powers or not, why not try focusing on your gemstones by holding them, and then at the same time imagine and concentrate on your desire, your dream, your ultimate goal. See it achieved within your mind's eye; believe there is someone or something listening, and that, just like a 'helpline' with an answering machine, they will respond as soon as they can, and help you in ways you probably couldn't even imagine. Allow your gemstone-crystals to act like a catalyst or sub-station to help boost your natural energy - an energy found within the human experience, within the mind.

How to produce a lucky talisman.

**You don't need to know how a telephone works
to make a phone call - only how to speak!**

To make a talisman, there must be a link, a bridge, to join with the 'universal life force' and the recipient. The talisman here is like the phone: acting as a catalyst, helping to bring these two things together. The more symbolic the ritual. the more it will bring about a connection.

A white cloth (handkerchief), a glass of water, a few grains of common rock or sea salt, a white candle and an incense stick are all you need to produce the most powerful, supercharged talisman.

Lay out the white cloth, then light the candle and incense stick. Clear your mind. Relax. Start thinking what you would like your talisman to achieve. Then imagine the desired end result; actually see it in your mind's eye. Believe, expect and let your subconscious - now helped by your imagination, in the form of your talisman - bring it to fruition.

Start this symbolic ritual. with expectancy. Although the 'universal life force' is invisible, nevertheless it is very real, and you are about to ask for its help. You are a child of the Universe; claim your inheritance.

The ritual.
Start by laying your white cloth on the table and placing your glass of water onto it. Imagining the glass of water filled with a golden light. Take a pinch of salt and slowly watch the granules fall into the water. Use your fingers to sprinkle the salty water onto your Gem-Crystal Talisman, whilst still imagining the golden light shining in the water.

Next, pass your Talisman through the smoke from the incense stick to symbolically purify it. Hold it there for a short while, and then pass your talisman through the flame of the candle, which symbolises the cleansing away of all the impurities. Your Talisman, having now been cleansed, is ready to be 'charged'.

Take your Talisman, close your eyes and hold it in your passive hand so as to receive. Start to imagine a sphere of golden light radiating from above in all directions, just like a small sun. Concentrate all your energy into this sphere and by using your imagination, start to feel its power and brilliance grow.

Imagine a beam of golden light being directed from it, and being focused onto the top of your head. Imagine it descending through your body and into the ground. Feel the heat, the warmth and the energy, just as you would feel the sudden warmth of the sun as it comes out from behind a cloud.

Now imagine a second beam of light. The colour's changed to white, and it is being directed from your solar plexus directly towards your Talisman. Start to imagine your desire or object that you are wanting to achieve. Hold the thought for a moment, and then let go; relax. Your Talisman is now fully charged and beginning to work for you, in perfect harmony with 'Universal Life'.

Be prepared for positive changes - they are about to come.

To protect yourself from any random negative energy whilst performing the above ritual, it would be wise, before you start, to 'affirm' with a prayer. Here's an example:

*'I ask only the highest forces of God, my higher self or my guides
and angels to work through this Talisman.
This I ask in the name of Love and for the good of all'.*

As with any sincere practice of prayer, visualisation, ritual or magic, the power comes from the intention - that wise connection between the self and that which is divine, the 'Universal Life Force'.

Live the journey - the journey is Life.

See your local stockist first, for any Gemstones and Crystals mentioned in this publication. If you are having difficulty obtaining any of the stones mentioned, we do offer our own mail order service and would be more than pleased to supply any of the stones listed in the form of Tumblestones. These are smooth, rounded stones ideal for use as Birthstones or as Healing Crystals.

For further details - write to:
Rosewood
P.O. Box 219, Huddersfield, West Yorkshire. HD2 2YT

E-mail enquiries to: info@rosewood-gifts.co.uk

Or why not visit our website for even more information:

www. rosewood-gifts.co.uk

A Guide into
The Mysteries Surrounding
Gemstones and
Crystals

Crystal Healing – Birthstones – Crystal Gazing
Lucky Talismans – Elixirs – crystal Dowsing
Astrology – Rune Stones – Amulets
Rituals

By
Robert W. Wood D.Hp
(Diploma in Hypnotherapy)

Rosewood Publishing

BK10

A Guide to the Mysteries surrounding
Gemstones and Crystals

'The greatest Mystery of them all is life itself; and we are the privileged to have been invited to experience it.'

Introduction.
From the very beginning, man has always been excited about the possibilities of life. Over the years he has used one of the greatest gifts that God could give, other than life itself. He has been given an amazing power: the gift of imagination. Imagination has enabled man to explain and demonstrate, and has helped him to mystify and entertain his fellow humans.

There can't be a greater collection of mysteries than those surrounding Gemstones and Crystals. Even the fact that Gemstones and Crystals exist is in itself a mystery. Somehow built within themselves is their 'genetic code' – their DNA – and this has not changed since the beginning of time. Gemstones therefore are the backbone of life, of Mother Earth and her children.

In man's quest to understand life, he's never been shy in using whatever tools were available. From the oldest knowledge to the very latest ideas such as Crystal Dowsing, healing crystals have played a part. It's only now that we are beginning to discover the truth behind theses mysteries, and we may only now be reaching an understanding of how all this works – of why and how crystals have helped man grow, over the years. By researching and by using all our understanding of life itself, we may be closer than ever to understanding why these things were cloaked in secrecy and concealed; and why only now are we being given an understanding.

'I will utter things hidden since the creation of the world'
MATT. 13 – 35

Using all available sources of Knowledge including all the known religions, Philosophy, psychology, science and the work of psychics and mystics, we are able to gain a unique insight into the mysteries. The discovery of light frequencies, energy waves, microwaves and quantum physics all have helped.

The following pages are a guide into many of these mysteries. We start with probably the oldest known to man – Healing crystals.

Crystal Healing.

Crystals and Gemstones have always been highly prized, not only because of their colour or beauty but also for their healing and spiritual properties. Science has yet to discover what actually occurs during crystal healing, and yet this in no way diminishes the fact that real changes are clearly felt by many. Placing a crystal close to an energy imbalance (an illness), whether it's physical or emotional, seems to encourage our own healing process to become activated.

The Sages, very often the High Priests, were revered for their profound wisdom and knowledge. Without the advantages of our modern knowledge and drugs, they had to discover and use more natural remedies for healing the sick. Their skills must have seemed astounding to their people. They had to rely entirely on natural elements to effect their cures and bring about relief for many kinds of illness.

These 'wise men' were drawn to crystals, maybe because of their colour, purity or even shape, but they obviously felt that crystals had special powers. In today's frantic, stressful and busy world, many people are seeking an alternative lifestyle. Many are turning once again back to Mother Nature and the mineral kingdom, to see if they can discover the healing properties of crystals for themselves. This is one explanation for the upsurge in the number of people wanting to know more, and the reason behind the popularity of the many 'crystal healing workshops'.

By simply holding or wearing a crystal, or even just by being near to one, people have often found a long-lasting beneficial effect; a feeling of calm, of being less agitated, of being energised, revitalised, and in many cases even completely healed. According to the holistic healers, when we are ill we are out of balance with nature, and a crystal, being pure and energised with the power of the earth and the power that created it, can help to guide us back into balance. A little like if a radio station goes off station; what do we do? We retune it in, until it's in tune, back on station. In our case, we're brought back into health.

It's exactly the same as the explanation given for swimming with dolphins: just being near a dolphin can, for many, have amazing beneficial effects. And it's said to be exactly the same with Gemstones and Crystals.

Crystal Healing (continued)
When I give my talk on the mysteries surrounding gemstones and crystals, I often demonstrate crystal healing, and I must say with some amazing effects. As a Christian I always explain that you wouldn't dream of worshipping aspirin just because it may help with a headache, so I am not for a moment suggesting anybody worships stones. It's just that they didn't have aspirin years ago and so it was crystals that they used.

In fact there is plenty of evidence to suggest that they used a whole range of crystals to effect cures. These cures using crystal healing techniques have, for many, achieved spectacular successes. How? Going back in time, the priests knew that crystals could bring great benefit to the health of their people. How? We can still only guess at the explanations.

All crystals, gemstones and minerals contain trace elements, and our bodies need trace elements to function correctly. Over the centuries, folklore and family traditions were passed down through the generations, and from this knowledge came the idea of gemstones and crystals being crushed and dispensed as cures for many ailments. Although the idea of being cured by a lump of rock may sound crazy in the modern world, it's said that crystals have been doing just that since the dawning of time.

Scientific research has shown an amazing fact: that crystals vibrate at different frequencies. For example, a digital watch works because a small piece of quartz vibrates at a constant frequency when stimulated by the energy from a battery.

Experts believe that our bodies act like a watch battery, and that we can stimulate crystals in such a way that they can have this beneficial effect towards our well-being. To put it simply: if we place a crystal close to us, our bodies will tune into the crystal's frequency and vibrations. In effect the crystal will energise and heal us by activating within us our own healing system. Sometimes we just need a little extra help. It's like tuning into the different channels on a radio; you can tune it in for health, energy, peace of mind etc. Whatever it is we need, there will be a crystal that's said to be able to help. It's just a case of finding the right crystal or crystals.

I know many say you have to believe in it, and if that means by believing in it, it works, then believe in it. Thought patterns create energy, and it may be that positive thoughts are being amplified with the help of crystals. In truth we still don't know how it works; but for many, it does; so keep an open mind.

The 'Rune Stones'.

This is the name given to the characters or symbols of an ancient Germanic alphabet in use, especially in Scandinavia, from around the third century AD to the end of the Middle Ages.

Runes consist of a set of ancient signs or symbols, each one traditionally marked onto a small flat stone, either carved, painted or drawn. Today, most Rune users work with a Rune alphabet of twenty-four symbols. Runes are an ancient tool for divination, and later also acted as lucky talismans by helping guard and protect, as well as their original use, to guide. Outside those of Scandinavian descent, probably few people have even heard of the word 'Rune'; and although there's no way of knowing exactly when, where or why the Runes originated, research has shown we could be going further back than 300 AD, even to around 2,000 years ago, to around the time of Jesus Christ.

A Norse legend tells that the mysteries of the Runes were revealed to Odin, the god of magic. His insatiable appetite for greater knowledge drove him to search for power and meaning. The legend tells of an initiation ceremony of shamanic proportions, where he obtained the power and meaning of the Runes. In order to acquire the secrets of the Runes, a knowledge he wanted to share with everyone, he meticulously took his own life in a slow process that lasted nine days and nine nights, by hanging from a tree, enduring pain, hunger and thirst. At the very moment of death he gained an insight into his quest, giving him the secret knowledge. He was then resurrected, enabling him to share the knowledge and secrets of the Runes with others. Fortunately for us, we don't need to undergo the same torments as Odin did.

The word 'Rune' is derived from an Old Norse term for 'secret'. The Runes enjoyed the height of their popularity during the Viking era, when they were used extensively as tokens of magical power. The Vikings, who first attacked Britain in 793 AD, earned themselves a reputation for bloodshed and destruction, and their ideas may have been philosophically a long way away from the original concept behind the Runes.

Originally, Runes were firmly grounded in the natural world and not the magical. They were symbols of the power exhibited by the different elements of nature. Then Norse mythology built on this knowledge embedding into the Runes the ancient Norse beliefs and energies.

Rune Stones – a deeper meaning.

It's important to realise that a reading using the Rune stones has nothing to do with having you fortune told. It's more like a visit to a psychoanalyst. The Runes are a tool to help you tune into you own inner wisdom. They guide our thoughts towards our deepest hidden fears and emotions, our dreams and our ambitions.

Once we have discovered these then we are in a much stronger position to reshape our future. That's because being aware of our inner struggles from the past gives us a knowledge that can free us from bondage and help explain what has been secretly misshaping and influencing our lives, here in the present. Once aware of these elements, which are found within the psyche, we can then re-direct our thoughts and alter our future choices, thus becoming the master of our own destiny.

How Runes would be used.
It's quite simple to make a set of Runes. Just find twenty-four small flat stones or pieces of wood, and paint or draw on them twenty-four symbols (easily found on the internet).

Then put the Runes into a bag. Now you need a 'background'; this is a cloth with three circles drawn on it - like the R.A.F. symbol, the one that looks like a target. The inner circle represents the 'self'; the middle represents 'influences'; and the outer, 'future events'.

There are various ways of 'casting the Runes', as well as variations in the number of Runes used to cast. It's usual to cast in numbers of three, six or nine. Say you choose six, then this is how it would be done: Shake the Runes in the bag, and at the same time formulate a clear question within your mind. Then pick out six Runes. Then, still 'holding' the question within the mind, drop the six Runes onto the background. It's where and how they land that gives the opportunity to interpret their message, using your intuition and psychic imagination. Wow! Is that what they did nearly 2,000 years ago?

Astrology.
It all started around 6,000 years ago, when ancient Man first settled down. The Sumerians, who settled in Mesopotamia around 4,000 BC, mark the first example of a people who worshipped the Sun, Moon and Venus. They considered these heavenly bodies to be gods, or the homes of gods. The priests of the time who 'communicated' with the gods were the first rulers. Temple systems were created, together with staff; several thousand people were 'employed' in different roles to fulfil various needs.

The earliest civilisations, such as the Babylonians, the Egyptians and even the Chinese, believed that the stars and planets influenced their lives. The Babylonians, in particular, thought that the position of the stars and planets represented coded messages from the gods and so they observed and plotted the night sky with great care and in great detail.

Studying in this way, they were able to produce very accurate maps that recorded the position of the stars in relationship to the time of the year. They were able to correlate the seasons with the rotation of the earth, the moon and the sun – the birth of a science we now call Astrology.

It may be useful to make the distinction here between astrology and astronomy.

Astronomy is the scientific study of the stars and planets and their movements. Astrology is the pseudo-scientific study of the influence those heavenly bodies and their movements have on humankind.

The Assyrian era marked a new phase in the development of astrology, around 1,300 to 600BC. The Assyrians plotted eighteen constellations. By 600 BC, some of these had been combined and some had been deleted to form twelve constellations of the Zodiac. The Greeks influence on astrology started around the fifth and fourth centuries BC. The Greeks were responsible for incorporating mythology into astrology, and naming the now-familiar twelve signs of the Zodiac.

In 331BC Alexander the Great founded the city of Alexandria, and by the time the city went into decline, astrology was accepted and believed by almost everyone. After about 500AD, astrology died away for a while. It came alive again in the eighth century when Islam began practising Hellenistic astrology. It was Albumasar, a Muslim intellectual, who was instrumental in bring astrology as we know it in the Western world.

Birthstones
The Sumerians were probably the first to relate gemstones to the planet Earth and the solar system. They were cutting and polishing softer gemstones such as Rock Crystal, Amethyst and Agates. These were used extensively to decorate their buildings and artefacts, to add splendour and majesty. Members of royal families also wore gemstones set in silver as jewellery, as a sign of status.

The Greeks believed that gemstones, like humans, were born under the influence of the planets. For example, a person born under the sign of Pisces shared that sign with the gemstone Amethyst. It's believed that birthstones were originally given to a new-born child, maybe in the form of a pendant or a loose stone, so as to protect the child from harm and attract to it good fortune.

To find twelve authentic Birthstones has meant scrutinising numerous different birthstones lists, many published by world-famous astrologers. I read, with great interest, articles in several encyclopaedias, and studied the Old and New Testaments of the

Bible. I consulted various New Age publications – in fact, any relevant article in ancient books and modern magazines. I finally came up with my list of twelve authentic birthstones:

Aries - **RED JASPER**; Taurus – **ROSE QUARTZ**; Gemini – **BLACK ONYX**; Cancer – **MOTHER OF PEARL**; Leo – **TIGER EYE**; Virgo – **CARNELIAN**; Libra – **GREEN AVENTURINE**; Scorpio – **RHODONITE**; Sagittarius – **SODALITE**; Capricorn – **OBSIDIAN SNOWFLAKE**; Aquarius – **BLUE AGATE**; and finally Pisces – **AMETHYST**.

In the Bible, in Exodus, there's a story of a Breastpiece and a list of twelve stones. These twelve stones symbolically represent the twelve tribes of Israel. In astrology, twelve stones represent the astrological cycle of life and are called Birthstones.

Another list of twelve stones appears in the New Testament, this time representing the New Jerusalem. It says the city walls were decorated with every kind of precious stone. The first foundation was Jasper – the gemstone I had picked for Aries, the first foundation in astrology. The sixth was Carnelian – the same as for the sixth sign, Virgo. And finally, the twelfth foundation of the New Jerusalem was Amethyst – the same I had picked for the twelfth sign, Pisces. Simply, a Birthstone acts as a lucky Talisman.

Lucky Talismans and Amulets.
Talismans – Any object that's believed to be endowed with magical powers is a talisman. Often it is a stone or other small object, sometimes inscribed or carved on, believed to protect the wearer from bad luck, evil influences, mischief or ill health. The item is active when it bestows this magical power upon the one who possesses it. Throughout history, magical talismans have been used to help bring protection, power and prosperity to their wearer or owner. They are specifically designed and energised to achieve a particular purpose, and work by generating a positive energy that can help to achieve this. Remember the story of Jack and the Beanstalk; it was the beans that were magical because they had been supercharged to grow into something very special – a giant Beanstalk.

Who can forget the sword Excalibur that gave King Arthur magical powers to win? During the time of the crusades, the Nordic countries employed their special magical alphabet known as the Runes for protection.

The word 'talisman' comes from the Greek word 'telesma', meaning 'to consecrate or magically charge'. As an example of the need to 'charge' a talisman, imagine a piece of bone. It wouldn't have any power; but when charged – and only then – this simple piece of bone would become a talisman.

Amulets – Unlike talismans, amulets do not need to be 'charged'. They come already imbued with their own built-in power for health, wealth, energy, good luck and so on. There is a certain 'passiveness' associated with the powers of an amulet, the possessor only needing to 'connect' by carrying, wearing or being near to it. The word 'amulet' is derived from the Latin 'amuletum', and may also have come from the Arab term 'hamala', which means 'to carry'. A good example of an amulet would be the Shamrock, which is a symbol of good luck – 'the luck of the Irish'.

The function of a talisman or amulet is to make things possible, to bring about powerful transformations, to help a person who would not feel confident within themselves, without a little help. So a talisman or amulet can initially be that help. It is a useful tool. It's a little like phoning a helpline – you have a problem and you need help; except there's no one there to take your call, only an answering machine. So you leave a message and hope that somehow, someone will listen and then get back to you with help later. In this analogy, the phone represents the talisman. It's the tool; it's the way of connecting to the helpline.

Talismans … Amulets
Our journey through life is all about personal empowerment and freedom of choice, and what we do with it. Throughout the history of humanity, people have placed their hope in inanimate objects, in the belief that they are gaining that extra little help. Whether you are a believer in the supernatural or not, gaining a sense of control over the uncontrollable is one explanation of why many people seem to

believe in lucky talismans. This belief crosses all nationalities, intelligence, education and status.

Luck may be an illusion of control, but control is what we seek in a random world. Although it may have no basis in science, it certainly can affect how we feel. Talismans and amulets can give a sense of preparedness, a feeling of control and a more positive outlook on life, which in itself may give us that edge to help improve our lives for the better.

There is a long tradition throughout history of talismans being made by alchemists, shamans, holy men, witches and priests. Alchemical talismans and amulets were often worn by kings and queens, diplomats and merchants, popes and bishops. The less expensive amulets, usually made by witches, were worn or hung in the house by nearly everybody else. The most common amulets were those that protected against violence, plague, theft and bad luck. Thinking about it, not a lot has changed. We are still wanting protection against violence, plague, theft and bad luck – only now we can include mugging, road rage, drug dealers, extortionists, rapist and child molesters. Here's a tip I heard from a woman who had had her car broken into a couple of times: she bought a Tiger Eye gemstone and left it in the car for protection – the 'eye of the Tiger'. "Has it worked?" I asked. "I haven't been broken into since," was her reply.

Maybe it's the belief that something will work that makes it work. Sometimes I hear people say, "It's mind over matter" – we have all heard it said – or "You have to believe in it". I have some thoughts on this; you'll have to read my book 'Discover why Crystal Healing Works' for more information (available from the publisher, details at the back of this book). But just imagine if all you had to do was to believe something worked, and then it did. Actually you may be surprised to find that for many this is exactly what seems to happen. We all need something to believe in, be it a faith, a lucky mascot, a talisman or a philosophy. There is a 'Universal Life Force' that many call God, and I believe one day we will discover that all the different roads of life lead ultimately back to the one source.

Crystal Dowsing.

Dowsing is a very simple skill which can be used by anyone to help them to connect with their own inner wisdom. It's an ancient Knowledge for unlocking psychic power, a natural force that can help with health, wealth, love, energy and success. Generally, it involves using a crystal pendulum and asking simple questions to which the answer can only be a 'yes' or a 'no'. Dowsing has its roots in ancient times, and was originally used for water divining when human survival depended on finding water. Today it's used more for spiritual guidance, health advice and even business decisions.

At its simplest, crystal dowsing involves asking questions to help seek out information not readily available by any other means. How does it work? It seems that the dowser creates a bridge between the logical and the intuitive parts of the brain – that is: the conscious (logical) and the subconscious (intuitive). Our consciousness could be easily compared to the visible part of an iceberg, which is only a tiny part of the whole. In fact nine-tenths of an iceberg is below the surface. Some have described tapping into this 'inner world', the world of the subconscious, as being like tapping into a rich vein of pure gold.

Dowsing therefore becomes an external expression of the internal. It's the visible 'bringing together' of the mind and the spirit. Although dowsing may be thought of as an art or even a science, it is really more 'holistic' – that is, it creates links between mind, body and spirit.

When we ask our 'dowsing question', we are asking our intellectual, rationally-thinking, conscious part of the mind. We ask a clear, unambiguous question in our mind. Then, having asked, we wait for the reply – a little like waiting for an internet search. The answer, when it comes, is in the form of movement. The crystal pendulum will begin to move either from side to side or from back to front, or even circling clockwise or anti-clockwise. This is the external expression of our inner world – the inner world of the subconscious – where you'll find intuition, our sixth sense.

For fun, why not try out crystal dowsing? If you haven't got a crystal, a key tied to the end of a piece of string will do.

Hold the pendulum so it's free to swing, and whatever you do, don't move. Then imagine the pendulum moving in any direction you want, and see what happens. The effect can be quite surprising.

Elixirs.
In homeopathy, plant or flower extracts are dissolved into a solution. The mixture is then strained, and the resulting solution is known as the 'mother tincture'. The mother tincture is then diluted with a mixture of water and alcohol, and is diluted again and again until there is no evidence of the original solution, and yet it still remains effective. This has led many to believe that somehow the 'memory' of the original solution still remains; and it's the same explanation for gemstones and crystal elixirs.

When we place a crystal or combination of crystals into water and then leave them overnight, the elixir solution that remains will somehow 'take on board' the memory of the crystals. If these crystals have been 'programmed' by nature to help bring about a desirable effect, then it seems that taking a sip of the elixir solution will have a beneficial affect; and if this is done in a ritualistic manner then its effect will be heightened. Simply: a gemstone elixir is water into which a gemstone-crystal has been placed and left, until the 'memory' of its health-giving or luck-changing vibrations is all that remains after the crystals have been removed.

Warning! Some gemstones are unsuitable for producing elixirs, particular those that are soluble. Some should not be used under any circumstances as they contain poisonous toxins. So be careful, and always take advice.

Gemstones and crystals have always been linked with Love, Health, Wealth, Prosperity, Energy and Success. Born from alchemy – a forerunner to our modern day chemistry – elixirs, lotions and potions were in times past only practised by a select few: priests, sages, holy men and magicians. Among these select few was Hildegard of Bingen. She was one of the many famous recorded purveyors associated with gemstone elixirs.

Hildegard of Bingen (1098-1179) was one of the outstanding females of the twelfth century.

From the time she was a young girl Hildegard experienced visions. Some of her ideas about gemstones can be traced back to the Roman naturalist Pliny and even earlier authors such as Aristotle (Fourth century BC). Many of her instructions or recipes involved the preparation of elixirs or the wearing of a stone, especially on the bare skin; soaking the stones in water or wine and then drinking the liquid or pouring it over the troubled spot. She claimed that angels described to her the healing properties of at least twenty-five stones. She describes putting a stone into water and on the fourth day using it to cook food for the one who was suffering. Elixirs have been around a long time.

Crystal Gazing.
During my research I came across the writings of John Dee. It's one of the earliest records, and it shows how he popularised crystal gazing in the 16th century. Dee was a contemporary of the Nostradamus, and, like Nostradamus, was an official astrologer for the Queen. The son of a minor official at the English court of Henry VIII, Dee was something of a child prodigy because of his early enthusiasm for browsing through books and manuscripts, and was driven by a quest to 'complete his knowledge'.

He maintained throughout his life that he possessed absolutely no occult faculties. By the age of nineteen he was a fellow of Trinity College, a gifted astronomer and a Catholic by faith. He was influenced by Cornelius Agrippa's occult philosophy and was excited by the notion that magic and alchemy were a practical aid in the mystical approach to God. While magic wasn't over-popular, it's worth noting that magic and science were linked in the sixteenth century.

In 1552 Dee met the occultist Jerome Carden, who practised with a very high degree of second sight, and this led Dee to the idea that spirits thrived just beyond the human realm and could be contacted to aid him in his research. Casting horoscopes for the rich and powerful became his passion, and soon he became the English court's Royal Astrologer. He did readings for Mary Queen of Scots and her sister Elizabeth.

From his stargazing he moved into glass-gazing using a mirror, and even gained some credit for England defeating the Spanish Armada in 1588

In his middle years he was busy 'entertaining' a steady parade of various 'spirits', 'guides' and 'messengers', and speaking from his Catholic experience he assumed them to be 'angels'. One vision he had identified an angel as 'Urief'. In its hand was a crystal egg. Then the Archangel Michael appeared and persuaded him not to fear, but to pick up the egg.
Strangely, there is a crystal egg or ball from John Dee currently on display in the British Museum.

Crystal ball gazing comes under the title of 'Intuitive Divination'. It's one of the more familiar of the intuitive types of divination. Everyone has come across the gypsy fortune-teller stereotype in the movies and on television, and surprisingly, in reality, this image is not that far off the mark. To perform this type of divination you need a crystal ball. Your mood and the lighting are very important in getting a good reading. A quiet candlelit area, free from distractions, tends to work best.

To begin, you should settle down to enter into a light trance. This can be done quite easily by concentrating on your breathing. Breath deeply and regularly for a minute or two, then try this method: see a red '7' in your imagination, then change it to an orange '6', a yellow '5', a green '4', a blue '3', a purple '2' and finally a violet '1'. It works well in bringing about an altered state of awareness. You could just count from 10 down to 1, and say in your mind after each number, "Going deeper now", alternating this with, "Going deeper than before". If you use these methods then, when you want to return to full consciousness, simply count from 1 to 5 and the fifth number say, "Feeling fine now, feeling wide awake, feeling better than before". These techniques also double up as very easy relaxation exercises and can be very beneficial. There are many other ways to enter into a trance. Just find the one that best suits you, and use it.

One way to describe what you are trying to do is this.

Imagine that you are looking at a pond of calm, clear water; see the reflection in the water of the surrounding trees, hills and mountains; even see the reflection of the clouds in the sky on the pond's surface. Then shift your gaze and go through the surface reflection, and now see the small fish swimming around; and looking deeper you can see the sand and rocks on the bottom. This is what you are trying to achieve – to see through the surface reflection.

As you look into your crystal ball, beyond the surface reflection, focus your mind on what it is that you wish to know, then formulate the question within your mind. It's worth noting that the conscious mind sometimes plays tricks and may send wish-fulfilling answers. If this happens, stop and try again. If you are inquiring about a lost friend or missing article, see the person or object in your minds eye and let the image dissolve. The first sign that something is happening will be a clouding of the crystal. It may seem to be filled with a milky-white mist that swirls around within the crystal ball. Relax; keep gazing; some seers, but not all, say that the milkiness changes to different colours. Eventually it will turn black. Then images and symbols will seem to appear, and these images will somehow relate to your question. Eventually the messages will seem to dissolve and the connection will be broken. At this moment, cover your crystal with a soft cloth, and this will mark the end of the gazing session. Then let your intuition guide your thoughts towards an explanation of the meaning of the message.

Gemstone-Crystal Rituals.
Once we have found a crystal or gemstone – and some say it may be more a matter of the stones finding us, rather than us them – there are one or two practical rituals that we should perform. The first is to cleanse it. This isn't a bad idea when you consider the number of people who may have touched or handled it. There is a school of thought that says stones can hold negative energy or imbalances and that cleansing or washing removes this, wiping them clean so as to restore them to their original clarity. Some go as far as to suggest that cleansing should be done every time the stones have been used for healing.

There are many ways of cleansing. You could just simply hold the stone under the tap and then dry it.

170

You could hold it under running water for a few minutes and then place it in the sun to dry out. Placing stones onto a large crystal cluster will clean and energise them. You could hold the crystal in the smoke of an incense or smudge stick. Herbs and spices such as sandalwood, cedar, sage and frankincense are used for their purifying qualities. The vibrations of pure sound can energetically clean a stone; a bell, gong or tuning fork can be used for this purpose. You could take a deep breath and blow over the crystal whilst imagining that you are clearing away negativities. You could even bury the stone in the ground for twenty-four hours and let Mother Nature re-charge the crystal.

After the cleansing rituals you need to connect with the stone. How do you know if you are connected? If someone asks where your crystal or gemstone is and you don't know, then you are not connected; but if you do know where it is, then you are connected. If you lost the stone and didn't know, then you were not connected. To be connected you have to know where it is at any time, day or night. That's why some will put their crystal under their pillow and sleep on it. The ritual part would be if they consciously touched the stone just before they went to sleep. If they could do this again first thing in the morning, whilst coming out of sleep and before getting out of bed, then they would be connected.

Another ritual could be to have the stone in the lounge, and at the same time each day 'visit' the stone and touch it, or turn the stone three times, like winding up a clock. You could do this three times a day. In fact, the more ritualistic, the more connected. It's no coincidence that churches are full of rituals. Why? Because rituals can help us to connect. Why do we want to connect? So we can experience the benefits of being connected.

And Finally …
Over the years I have received many letters, phone calls and even e-mails, all relating to how a gemstone or crystal has helped in one way or another. I know some will say, "It's all in the mind," and others will say "You have to believe in it," whilst others still will say, "It's mind over matter," and many more might say, "It's all nonsense".

Whatever their viewpoint most people are willing to give gemstones and crystals a try. I suggest you keep an open mind.

In my book 'An Alternative View on Crystal Healing', you will find a story of how I was told, after five days of meditation at an 'inner child' workshop, that my life's mission was to 'de-mystify the mysteries'. Isn't life strange? Look at what I do for a living: I give talks on the mysteries surrounding gemstones-crystals, and I write on the subject.

During my talks on the mysteries that surround gemstones and crystals, I explain that there is a formula – 'When imagination and willpower are in conflict, then imagination will always win'. It's set in granite. Take my word for it: it works. Once you have grasped the meaning, it can change your life forever. Willpower will not force a crystal to work, but the imagination can. You have a power beyond imagination. Learn how to use it; and let the 'magic' of life begin.

Live the journey – the journey is Life

For further details – write to:
Rosewood
P.O. Box 219, Huddersfield, West Yorkshire. HD2 2YT

E-mail enquiries to: info@rosewood-gifts.co.uk

Or why not visit our website for even more information:

www.rosewood-gifts.co.uk

From an Agate to a Zircon
A Comprehensive Guide to …

Gemstone and Crystal Power

A Mystical
A to Z of stones

By
Robert W. Wood D.Hp
(Diploma in Hypnotherapy)

Rosewood Publishing

BK11

From an Agate to a Zircon:
A Comprehensive Guide to
Gemstone and Crystal Power

A Guide ...

. . . a book that instructs or explains the fundamentals of a subject or skill.

Gemstones and Crystals.

Suffer from headaches? Why not try a Rose Quartz. Have a bad back? Then add Hematite to your Rose Quartz. It's said that together they can work wonders on aches and pains. In physics it's well known that the energy in iron ore (Hematite) helps to boost the energy of the Quartz. If it's a very bad back then add Rock Crystal (a clear Quartz) to the combination. It acts as a catalyst to help increase the healing power and energy of the other two minerals, Rose Quartz and Hematite.

Can't sleep? No problem - put an Amethyst under your pillow, and you'll sleep like a log. Prefer to stay awake and have a bit of fun? Then add a Carnelian. Feeling a little 'naughty'? Then add Rose Quartz; it's our 'Adults Only' combination, designed for nights of passion. But do remember to watch out for that bad back.

It all sounds weird, doesn't it? 'Impossible,' I can hear you saying, 'there's no way any of this can work.' Think again. Did you know that in the medical profession there's a well-known phenomenon called a 'placebo effect'? This occurs when patients are given a dummy medicine, a sugar-coated pill. It's based on a lie, and yet many have benefited and have even been totally cured. And so just as the placebo effect has to have its sugar-coated pill, so then the crystal healer has to have a crystal.

If you thought Gemstones and Crystals were just lumps of rocks, you're in for a pleasant surprise. They are nature's little treasures, and have been around for a very long time. In fact they have been around as long as time itself, and a lot longer than any chemists.

This book has been written to help those who are interested in alternative treatments, treatments without the side-effects that drugs can have. However, common sense should tell you to see your doctor or practitioner first, before embarking on any kind of alternative treatment.

The information that follows is in direct response to those that would like to know more, and is part of a series of books called 'Power for Life' - a series of books based on the mysteries surrounding gemstones and crystals; a refreshing view of an ancient wisdom. Keep an open mind and you won't go far wrong.

There are numerous ways of looking into the strange, often mystical world of gemstone and crystal powers, and you'll discover that there are many ways of explaining these mysteries too. I have spent many years researching into all the aspects of crystal power, in the search for a more modern explanation of why, once we are connected to a crystal, that crystal - or the connection - can actually be so beneficial to its user. The following information is only a 'taster' of a very large and complex subject. Before you think of dismissing all this as just hocus-pocus, think about this: at the heart of every computer are silicon chips, and what are they? They're a clear Quartz. A crystal. And crystals have power.

Believing in it.
It's often said that you have to believe in all this for it to work. But for years now, whenever I have been demonstrating crystal healing, I have always asked my audience not to believe in it, but to see what happens to them when I pass around a Rose Quartz and Hematite - a combination of stones said to work wonders on aches and pains. What better way to demonstrate and research at the same time, than with a willing audience? An audience that is just as curious as I am to see if stones do work, and if they can do what people say they can. In one year I gave over 200 talks and demonstrations, and I am no longer surprised at the number of people who tell me that they 'would never have believed it if they hadn't experienced it for themselves.' I wouldn't have known that they do work for so many, if I hadn't tried them out myself with all these audiences.

Apparently many find that their bad knees, backs, legs, necks and elbows, their headaches and their stiff joints do seem to benefit, or even be cured by this demonstration. Is it all in the mind? It's for you to decide; but remember this. In hypnosis, if you suggest to a person that the ice cube you have just placed in their hand is in fact a burning ember, once that thought strikes home then a blister will appear. On the other hand, think of a firewalker, walking on burning hot embers and not getting any blisters. 'Mind over matter' does exist.

Crystal power.

According to quantum physics, everything in the universe has an atomic structure - and that includes gemstones and crystals. They contain atomic energy, and this is the most powerful energy known on earth. Others talk of colour frequency. Red, orange and blue may seem to be different colours, but they are in fact all part of the same spectrum of light. Similarly, we tend to think of light, heat and radio waves as being different from each other, but there is a connection. The electromagnetic spectrum represents the complete range of radiation including gamma rays, X-rays, ultraviolet light, visible white light (visible to the human eye), infra-red light, microwaves and radio waves. Just because we can't see it, that doesn't mean it's not there - and it may be the same with gemstone and crystal power.

We can't hear dog whistles, but dogs can; we can't see ultraviolet light, but bees can. Just as our ears can only hear part of the range of possible sounds and cannot hear a dog whistle, so our eyes can only see a small central section of the electromagnetic spectrum of light. The power associated with Gemstones and Crystals falls into this 'can't be seen or heard' category.

Want to change your Luck?

Gemstones and Crystals have been used as lucky charms, amulets and talismans for thousands of years. Want to win the lottery? Then try a Green Aventurine - it's said to be a 'money magnet'. Or, if you play bingo, then try Obsidian Snowflake - it's a lucky talisman. Use a Tiger Eye (from South Africa) to take away your worries; or a Black Onyx to lose weight. It's the weight watchers' friend; it helps with self-control - we call it 'lose a stone'. Need to improve your memory? Then use a Rhodonite.

Within this book you'll find all the information you'll need about the metaphysical, astrological and physical properties of Gemstones, Crystals and minerals. I have scrutinised many sources and cross-referenced all the information to enable me to produce this guide. In short I have done all the work, so that you don't have to.

How to use this Guide.

The best way to use this Guide is to read the full list of Gemstones and Crystals starting on page 180, and at the same time make notes.

So, if you are looking for a healing stone for a specific ailment, read the full list, find the stone or stones, and if there are a few, then you might want to narrow them down. There are various ways of narrowing down. Trust your instincts on this one. For instance, you might find, from your research, two gemstone-crystals. It may be that for you, two are ideal. You may be surprised to find that one of the stones is your Birthstone; this would then be the one for you. Or if you have a favourite colour, and if that colour is there on your list, then go with that one. No-one is really sure how all this works; only that, for many, it does. Keep an open mind - many have been pleasantly surprised.

Colour - and the Chakras.

Another useful guide when choosing crystals could be their colour. In Sanskrit there are original teachings about an energy system known as the 'Chakras'.. When seen clairvoyantly, Chakras are wheels of light and colour. There are seven of them. The first one is found at the base or root - that is, around the base of the spine. The second is the sacral or spleen, the third is the solar plexus, and the fourth is the heart. The fifth is the throat, the sixth is the brow or 'third eye', and the seventh and final one is the crown. It's said we need all these energy centres to be open so as to enjoy optimum health. Each is associated with a colour; and these colours are the seven colours of the rainbow, and are in the same running order.

Each Chakra is linked with a particular colour in the spectrum of light. The 'root' Chakra is red; the 'sacral' or 'spleen' Chakra is orange; the 'solar plexus' Chakra is yellow; the 'heart' Chakra is green; the 'throat' Chakra is blue; the 'brow' Chakra is indigo; and finally the 'crown' Chakra is violet. I know it all may sound like gobbledygook, but the human body requires light to maintain itself. For example, our bodies produce vitamin D - necessary to make our bones and teeth strong and healthy - and this is increased as a result of exposure to sunlight. Think about this: where does the vitamin D come from? One minute it's not there and the next it is. What makes the difference? Stepping out into sunlight does - so light has a power, and you can use this knowledge to your benefit when choosing the right gemstones or crystals.

Cleansing Gemstones and Crystals.

Once you have found the right crystals and stones, it's advisable to clean them. This can quite easily be done by placing them under a running tap. Some say they should be washed in salt water; the sea is ideal, but if you're not near the sea then just add some salt to water. Others believe that gemstones and crystals can attract negative energy from other people, and, again, cleansing is a way of wiping them clean.

Whichever way you decide on, make it as ritualistic as you can; that is, do the cleaning with feeling. I know of some who will bury the stones in the ground for twenty-four hours, with the intention of allowing Mother Nature to put the energy back into the crystals. Others put the stones into a glass of water and place it in the window overnight to allow the moon to shine on it. Others place the stones onto larger clusters of crystals to be energised. There's no 'right' or 'wrong' way, only 'your' way.

Connecting to a crystal.

Once you've found your healing gemstone-crystal or your lucky talisman, your lucky charm or your birthstone, you have to connect with it. Remember the story of Aladdin and his three wishes? In the story, you'll remember, the Genie in the lamp was obliged to give three wishes to whoever owned the lamp; it didn't matter to the Genie who made the wishes. So before Aladdin could get his three wishes, firstly he had to own the lamp, and secondly he had to rub the lamp.

Here's the point: do you think if, in real life, you had Aladdin's lamp, there would ever be a time when you wouldn't know where it was? It's the same with your crystal. If at any time you are asked where it is and you don't know, then you are not connected. I am always being asked, 'How do I know if I am connected?' and the easiest answer I have found over the years is this: if you lost your crystal and didn't know you'd lost it, then you were not connected. Now enjoy the journey and find your special Gemstone.

Any information given in this book is not intended to be taken as a replacement for medical advice. If in any doubt, always consult a qualified doctor or therapist.

THE MYSTICAL A TO Z OF STONES.

AGATE ... The agate probably derives its name from the small river Achates in Sicily, but can be found in many places including Brazil, Madagascar and India. Its rich variations make it a beautiful, multi-faceted stone. A powerful healer, it restores body energy and eases stressful situations; gives courage and banishes fear; calms, and increases self-esteem. A stone for good health and fortune, it helps grounding and balance. A stabiliser.

AMAZONITE ... the 'thinkers' stone'. It aids creativity and improves self-worth. A confidence stone. It attracts money and success. A soothing stone; a giver of energy. Solid blue to turquoise, it works on the throat - the fifth Chakra. It inspires hope and is sometimes also called 'the hope stone'.

AMBER ... not a stone, but the fossilised resin of extinct pine trees. Good for the throat - the fifth Chakra. Worn by actors for good luck and a clear voice. Changes negative energy into positive and is often used as a lucky talisman. It helps the body to heal itself. It is calming, lifting heaviness and allowing happiness to shine through. It prolongs life with a clear the mind.

AMETHYST ... purple to dark violet, known by a variety of names: Bishop's Stone, Stone of Healing, of Peace, of Love. St. Valentine implied it was one of the best gifts between lovers. Aids creative thinking. Relieves insomnia when placed under the pillow. A powerful aid to spiritual awareness and healing. Helps with meditation, inspiration, intuition and divine love. A stone which helps to attract that special partner.

APACHE TEARS ... a variant of Obsidian, dark, smokey, translucent in colour. Good for grounding; transforms; aids in the release of deep emotions. Eases pain, loss and sadness. Neutralises negative magic.

APATITE ... blue in colour. Strengthens muscle tissue, aids co-ordination, assists with stuttering and hypertension, and helps to fight viruses. Can help with communications, especially after a misunderstanding.

AQUAMARINE ... a Beryl, clear blue-green. It represents an ocean of love. Preserves innocence, brings spiritual vision, calms the mind and lifts the spirits, releases anxiety and fear. It is recommended for those suffering a lot of grief. Gives insight and perception in dealings with people. Gives protection, often used as a good luck charm. Leads to greater self-knowledge, quickens the mind, promotes clear and logical thinking.

AVENTURINE ... a variety of Quartz, usually green with mica inclusions. Stabilises by inspiring independence, well-being and health. Acts as a general tonic on the physical level. If left in water overnight, it can then be used to bathe the eyes, and similarly to treat skin irritations. Encourages creativity, gives courage, independence, calmness and serenity. It is a money magnet and a good luck stone, a lucky talisman.

AZURITE ... deep blue to blue-purple. An aid for meditation, it is used to increase psychic powers as it helps to induce prophetic dreams, intuition and understanding. It's also known as the 'Decision Maker'. With its high copper content it assists the flow of energy throughout the nervous system, strengthens the blood and is used to treat arthritis and joint disabilities.

BERYL ... many colours. The best of the Beryl group are emeralds and aquamarines. In ancient rituals the Beryl was used to bring rain. It is related to the sea and guards its wearer against drowning and sea-sickness. Protects against 'mind games'. Helps to stimulate the mind, and increases confidence. In the sixteenth century, it was worn to win arguments and debates.

BLOODSTONE (Heliotrope) ... a form of Jasper - dark green in colour, with red flecks. The red flecks are symbolic of Christ's death and his blood spilling onto the stone. Acts on all of the Chakras, a physical healer and a mental balancer. Removes toxins and aligns energies, especially along the spinal cord. Helps prevent miscarriages and eases childbirth. Works to overcome depression and pain of the emotional kind. Calming, grounding and revitalising. A stone to attract wealth, often used in business or legal matters to help attract success.

CALCITE ... red, orange, yellow, green and blue (see the Chakras). There is also a clear variety of calcite called Iceland Spar which, when placed over a line on a piece of paper, will produce a double image. Calcite is a strong balancing stone, giving comfort and lifting depression. Also alleviates fear, aids mental clarity, calms turbulent emotions, expands awareness and aids intuition. Good for pancreas and spleen. Clears toxins by gently helping to cleanse the blood.

CARNELIAN (Cornelian) ... mainly bright orange. The 'friendly one' - it is a very highly evolved healer. A good balancer; can help you connect with your inner self. Good for concentration. Brings joy, sociability and warmth. Good for rheumatism, arthritis, depression, neuralgia, and helps to regularise the menstrual cycle. When coupled with amethyst, purifies consciousness, reverses negative thoughts and shakes off sluggishness.

CAT'S EYE ... golden to mid-yellow, green to bluish brown. The Greeks called it 'Cymophane' meaning 'wave-light'. It resembles the contracted pupil of a cat's eye. In the symbolic necklace of 'Vishnu' the green gem was held to represent the earth. A magnetic centre of human passions. It is used to increase beauty and wealth, to protect, and to guard against danger.

CELESTITE ... white to clear; light blue cluster crystals. Signifies honesty. Helps with tiredness, soothes nerves and stress. Quietens the mind, promotes compassion, expands creative expression, reveals truth.

CHALCEDONY ... soft blue, translucent, belonging to a large group of crystalline forms and geodes. Stimulates optimism and enhances spiritual creativity. Diminishes nightmares and fear of the dark. A stone that guards travellers, and helps grounding through negative times. Banishes fear, mental illness, hysteria and depression.

CHRYSOCOLLA ... blue to blue-green opaque mineral, essentially a copper-element mineral. 'The woman's friend', relieving tension, pains and problems, soothing period pains and pre-menstrual tension. Increases energy, wisdom and peace of mind. Alleviates feelings of guilt, clears all negativity and brings about patience and contentment. Helps to attract love.

CHRYSOPRASE ... an apple-green form of chalcedony, the colour being due to traces of nickel. For wisdom and meditation. Helps the wearer to see clearly into personal problems, especially sexual frustrations and depressions. Worn to lift the emotions, attract friends and shield against negativity.

CITRINE ... clear to yellow-orange. Natural citrine was originally amethyst, transformed by being reheated and burnt in the earth's crust. Helps to clear mental and emotional problems and improve memory. Enhances willpower, optimism and confidence. Helps those who feel they have lost their way in life and need to find a new sense of direction. Strengthens the immune system, improves poor circulation and aids tissue regeneration. Placing a single crystal or cluster into a safe, till or cash box helps to attract ever-increasing financial income.

COPPER ... mixes easily with other metals; for example, copper, tin and zinc make bronze.

Copper is thought to be one of the best transmitters of healing energy. This may be because it has been used very successfully against cholera; it was discovered that men who worked with copper didn't get cholera, and that wearing copper improves the metabolism, reduces inflammation and increases blood flow. Worn next to the skin it soothes arthritis and rheumatism and can kill all kinds of bacteria. Certain bacteria are found in plenty on silver coins but are said never to be found on copper.

CORAL ... red, pink or white. Calcium calcite was once a living sea creature and is therefore thought to contain 'life essence'. It is used as a protector, especially to safeguard children. Sometimes referred to as the 'Tree of Life of the Ocean', it protects and strengthens the wearer's emotional foundation. Also, because it symbolises fertility, it offers a defence against sterility.

DIAMOND ... a well-known mineral, the purest and hardest substance in nature. It forms the neatest and sharpest of all known cutting edges and is now used in microsurgery with spectacular effect. When used with loving, clear intent, it clears blockages and opens the crown Chakra. Amplifies the full spectrum of energies in the mind, body and spirit.

DIOPTASE ... deep blue to green. Rivals the Emerald in its beauty and holistic healing powers. It empowers the heart with new depth, strength, healthiness, courage, and the ability to love deeply again. Promotes genuine, sincere emotional balance, self-worth and deep well-being; helps heal sadness, heartache, abuse and neglect. A stone for the heart.

EMERALD ... green. An excellent general healer, used in ancient times as a blood detoxifier and anti-poison. Improves creativity, imagination, memory and quick-wittedness. Helps the intellect and improves intelligence. Gives power to see the future. Grants success in business ventures and offers patience, harmony, peace and prosperity. An emotional stabiliser.

FLUORITE (Fluorspar) ... appears in all rainbow colours. A 'new age' stone that strengthens thought and balances mental energy. Good for meditation. Fluorite clears the mind of stress and aids sleep. Helps physical and mental healing and strengthens bone tissue, especially tooth enamel. Relieves dental disease, viral inflammations and pneumonia.

GARNET ... black, pink-red, yellow-brown, orange or green. A member of a vast gemstone family. A 'knight in shining armour', contains a little of most metals but especially aluminium, silicon and oxygen.

A revitalising tonic for the whole body, creating a shield of positive energy; aids in dreams, past lives, self-confidence and personal courage, and attracts love.

GEODES ... are hollow volcanic bubbles containing crystals. All Quartz, Rock Crystal, Amethyst and Opal is formed within geodes. The effect is brought about by the mineral-rich watery fluids percolating into the cavity or hole left by the 'bubble' which occurred in the steaming red hot volcanic lava. Some geodes are huge enough to drive cars through, while others are small enough to fit in the palm of your hand.

HEMATITE ... a natural ferric oxide, a silver-grey metallic mirror-like stone. You either like or dislike it, there's no 'in between'. To those who like it, it's a very optimistic inspirer of courage and personal magnetism. It lifts gloominess and depression and, when used in conjunction with Carnelian, can prevent fatigue. Good for blood, spleen and generally strengthens the body. Effective during pregnancy; helps with stress.

JADE ... comes in a variety of colours. It's a money magnet, a good luck talisman, and a protector from accidents, evil spirits and bad luck. It encourages long life, safe journeys, wisdom, courage, peace and harmony. The geological term for Jade is Nephrite, from the Greek word 'nephros' meaning 'kidney'. As a healer, Jade is good for kidneys, bladder, lungs and heart; the immune system, and even high blood pressure.

JASPER ... chalcedony quartz. Multi-coloured. A popular talisman, well liked amongst psychic healers. Protects from all kinds of ailments. It's a powerful healing stone, invigorating and stabilising. It calms troubled minds and helps to slow down the ageing process. Helps those suffering from emotional problems by balancing the physical and emotional needs.

JET ... a black glass-like substance - fossilised wood, another type of coal, mainly from Whitby in England. Even the Jet used in ancient Mesopotamia was thought to have been originally mined in Whitby. Like amber, when rubbed it becomes electrically charged. A good travel aid. Helps increased psychic awareness, guards against witchcraft, demons, melancholy and anxiety, and is very good for manic-depressives.

KUNZITE ... pink to dark lilac-rose. Has a high lithium content. Named after Dr G F Kunz, a noted mineralogist. Good for both the emotional and spiritual heart; reduces depression and mood swings. When held, induces relaxation by releasing tension and stress. A balancer for mind, body and spirit. Benefits those with any kind of compulsive behaviour.

KYNITE ... light blue. Contains aluminium. It is softer lengthways than it is across, and is immune to the forces of other chemicals (such as acids). Brings out our natural ability to manifest things into reality via thoughts and visualisation. Encourages devotion, truth, loyalty and reliability.

LABRADORITE ... 'irridescent Feldspar'. Yellow, pink, green, blue and violet. When in trouble and in doubt, wear a labradorite. A stone for today, it opens the energy flow to any or all of the Chakra centres, whichever is in greatest need. Brings restful sleep and straightening of the spine.

LAPIS LAZULI ... medium to dark blue with gold pyrite flecks. Called by the ancient Egyptians 'the Stone of Heaven', and thought to be the stone upon which were carved the laws given to Moses. A stone for teachers; helps ease expression and gain higher wisdom and clarity. Good for mental, physical, spiritual, psychic and emotional problems, and well-known for healing the whole. Alleviates fear and eases depression, quiets the mind; helps with creativity, writing, dreams, insight, self-expression and finding inner truth.

MALACHITE ... dark and light bands of green tints. Its name probably comes from the Greek 'malache' ('mallow', as of the colour of a green mallow leaf). Egyptians used green Malachite paste for eye make-up. Stimulates physical and psychic vision and concentration. Contains copper and is useful in treating rheumatism and arthritis.
Good for raising the spirits, increasing health, hope and happiness. Brings prosperity and is used to guard against all negativity.

MOLDAVITE ... formed by a meteorite strike in the Moldau Valley area of the Czech Republic over twelve million years ago. A powerful healing stone, it helps telepathic access to spiritual laws, and attracts information from higher levels to help us and our earth to become healthier and more spiritual. Helps us to understand our true purpose in life. A stone of transformation.

MOONSTONE ... an opalescent Feldspar. In India the Moonstone is a sacred gem, thought to be lucky if given by the groom to his bride. Called the 'Travellers' Stone' because it was a favourite protective amulet for those going on perilous journeys. Claimed to promote long life and happiness. It soothes stress and anxiety and is good for period pains and other kindred disorders. A powerful fertility and good luck stone from India.

MOTHER OF PEARL ... is the lustrous, opalescent interior of various sea molluscs. Aptly dubbed the 'sea of tranquillity', it creates physical harmony of a gentle but persuasive kind. Calms the nerves. Indicates treasure, chastity, sensitivity and strength. Good for calcified joints and the digestive system. Relaxes and soothes the emotions; helps with sensitivity and stress. Carries the gentle, peaceful healing energy of the sea.

OBSIDIAN SNOWFLAKE ... not really a stone, but a volcanic glass. Also Obsidian Black, Mahogany and Clear. For all those it recognises, it's a powerful healer. Keeps energy well grounded, clears subconscious blocks and brings an insight and understanding of the power behind silence, detachment, wisdom and love. A very lucky talisman, a bringer of good fortune. Was favoured by ancient Mexican cultures to neutralise negative energy and black magic. Good for eyesight, stomach and intestines, and alleviates viral and bacterial inflammations.

ONYX ... black, 'lightweight' Quartz. It can give a sense of courage and help to discover truth. Instils calm and serenity; diminishes depression. Gives self-control whilst aiding detachment and inspiring serenity. A protective stone worn in times of conflict, a student's friend as it encourages concentration and protects against unwise decisions. It is often found in rosaries; it helps to improve devotion, and relieves stress.

OPAL ... a silica. The 'Rainbow Stone'. Multi-coloured, it is a wonderful stone to behold, and can be charged with virtually every type of energy needed. It controls temper and calms the nerves. It was sometimes considered unlucky, but (according to Thomas Nichols' book of 1652) this is probably why: 'Opalus:- cloudeth the eyes of those that stand about him who wears it, so that they can either not see or not mind what is done before them; for this cause it is asserted to be a safe patron of thieves and thefts.' Because of its beauty, things were stolen or went missing, hence, according to some, its unlucky label.

PERIDOT ... clear bright green, also green to yellow (Chrysolite). A good anti-toxin gem, for cleaning most organs and glands. An overall tonic. Used by the Egyptians, Aztecs and Incas to gently help cleanse and heal the physical, including heart, lungs, lymph and muscles. Prized by the Crusaders as 'their' stone. It clears energy pathways, strengthens the 'breath of life', and attracts prosperity, growth and openness. It's also useful for attracting love and opening new doors of opportunity and abundance.

RHODOCROSITE ... a solid to clear, beautiful pink stone. Good for giving and receiving love. Inspires forgiveness. Heals emotional scars; helps to cope with loneliness, loss, heartache, fears, insecurities and inner child issues. Helps prevent mental breakdown and balances physical and emotional traumas. Soothes and de-stresses the body, cheers the depressed and coaxes back the life force in the very sick.

RHODONITE ... pink with black inclusions. Improves memory, calms the mind and reduces stress. Gives confidence and self-esteem. Cheers the depressed, preserves youth and retards the ageing process. Helps to bring back the life force into the sick. Carries the power to the unobstructed love. Good for emotional trauma, mental breakdown, spleen, kidneys, heart and blood circulation. A very special stone.

ROCK CRYSTAL ... also known traditionally as Clear Quartz. This stone holds a place of unique importance in the world of gems. It enlarges the aura of everything near to it, by acting as a catalyst to increase the healing powers of other minerals. Its vibration resonates with the beat of life, giving Rock Crystal a key role in all holistic practices. Good for the mind and soul, strengthening, cleansing and protecting, especially against negativity.

ROSE QUARTZ ... translucent to clear pink. Possesses healing qualities for the mind. It can help with migraine and headaches. It excites the imagination, helps to release pent-up emotions, lifts spirits and dispels negative thoughts. Eases both emotional and sexual imbalances and increases fertility. Good for spleen, kidneys and circulatory system. Coupled with Hematite, works wonders on aches and pains throughout the whole body.

RUBY ... blood red. Plays a vital role in micro-surgery as a cauterising instrument. Used to alleviate all kinds of blood disorders, anaemia, poor circulation, heart disease, rheumatism and arthritis. Helps ease worries; lifts the spirits. Improves confidence, intuition and spiritual wisdom, courage and energy; produces joy, dispels fear and strengthens willpower. Gives strength in leadership and success over challengers.

RUTILATED QUARTZ ... clear Quartz which contains titanium oxide in the form of slender needles; these amplify the energy of the Quartz. It aids healing, eases bronchial problems and increases tissue growth. Also stimulates mental activity and eases depression, improves decisiveness, strength of will, and helps to communicate with the higher self.

SAPPHIRE ... related to Ruby. A range of colours, but best known and loved for the dark blue variety. Worn to stimulate the 'third eye', to expand wisdom during meditation. A sacred gem worn by kings to ward off evil.

Good for improving the state of mind, increasing clarity of thought and dispelling confusion. Calms the nerves, attracts good influences and strengthens faith. Reputed to lengthen life, keeping its wearers looking young. Fortifies the heart and is a guardian of love, feelings and emotions.

SMOKEY QUARTZ ... looks exactly as its name implies - smokey. A grounding stone. Ideal around electrical goods such as computers, because it disperses negative patterns and vibrations. It can draw out and absorb negative energies, replacing them with positive. Alleviates moods, depression and other negative emotions; protects against despair, grief and anger. Used in meditation, it helps explore the inner self by penetrating dark areas with light and love. A 'Dream Stone'.

SODALITE ... deep blue with veined white flecks; often mistaken for Lapis Lazuli, but lacks the golden flecks. Calms and clears the mind, enhancing communication and insight with the higher self. A good stone for people who are over-sensitive and defensive. Brings joy and relieves a heavy heart. When placed at the side of the bed it can make a sad person wake up full of the joys of spring. Imparts youth and freshness to its wearer. When coupled with Rhodonite it produces the 'Elixir of Life'.

TIGER EYE ... generally associated with yellow to chocolate-brown. An iridescent combination of colour, resembling the gleaming eye of a tiger at night. The stone has a shifting lustre of golden light across it. Inspires brave but sensible behaviour with great insight and clearer perception. Fights hypochondria and psychosomatic diseases. A true 'confidence stone'. It attracts good luck, protects from witchcraft, and is an ideal 'worry stone' (let the stone do the worrying). Always carry one for protection.

TOPAZ ... many different colours, the most popular being rose-red to pure white. Named after the island Topazion. Known as the 'abundant one'; a stone of strength; a charm against fires and accidents. Promotes good health by overcoming stress, depression, exhaustion, fears and worries. Good for soothing, tranquillising, calming and protecting.

TOURMALINE ... has a colour for all seven of the Chakras. A master physician from the mineral world, working on all Chakra levels. A strong protector against misfortune and misunderstandings, it attracts goodwill, love and friendships. It settles troubled minds, gives confidence, inspires, calms the nerves, expands mental energy and helps clarity of thought.

TURQUOISE ... an opaque, light blue to green mineral. A sacred stone to native American Indians, and a powerful talisman to the Egyptians and the Turkish. A Lucky Stone, a protector against radiation and dark forces; a talisman favoured by horse-riders. A good all-round general healer, gentle, cooling and soothing; a stone that brings wisdom and psychic connection to the Universal Spirit. Turquoise strengthens and aligns all Chakras and energy fields. An absorber of negativity, a guardian against failure and poverty.

UNIKITE ... usually green with red patches. A variety of granite. Its name is taken from the Unaka range of mountains in North Carolina, USA. Autumnal in colour, it is a beautiful stone. It helps the wearer to relax and find peace of mind. It works mainly on a higher plain rather than the physical, going beyond into the spiritual world to find truth, bringing an understanding the true cause of disease and discomfort.

ZIRCON ... from the Arabic word 'Zarkun' ('vermilion'). Similar to Diamond in lustre and colour and often used as a substitute for diamonds. Known as the 'stone of virtue', it strengthens the mind and brings joy to the heart. Represents vitality, and works with the 'crown' Chakra, helping to connect to Universal Truth. Good for intuition, integrity, insomnia and depression.

Birthstones

On the next page you will find a list of twelve Birthstones. In my research I studied over 17 different lists. My list is the same as the Bible's list for Aries, Virgo and Pisces.

These lists have been heavily researched. There are others. However, I believe the first list to be authentic. The second list gives the most popular precious stones for the United Kingdom; and the third list is taken from the Bible: a 'New Jerusalem'.

BIRTHSTONES

Zodiac Star signs	Semi-precious Stones	Precious Stones	Bible Rev. 21-19
ARIES (21 Mar - 20 Apr)	Red Jasper	Diamond	Jasper
TAURUS {21 Apr - 21May)	Rose Quartz	Emerald	Sapphire
GEMINI (22 May - 21 Jun)	Black Onyx	Pearl	Chalcedony
CANCER (22 Jun - 22 Jul)	Mother of Pearl	Ruby	Emerald
LEO (23 Jul - 23 Aug)	Tiger Eye	Peridot	Sardonyx
VIRGO (24 Aug - 22 Sep)	Carnelian	Sapphire	Carnelian
LIBRA (23 Sep - 23 Oct)	Green Aventurine	Opal	Chroysolite
SCORPIO (24 Oct - 22 Nov)	Rhodonite	Topaz	Beryl
SAGITTARIUS (23 Nov - 21 Dec)	Sodalite	Turquoise	Topaz
CAPRICORN (22 Dec - 20 Jan)	Obsidian Snowflake	Garnet	Chrysoprase
AQUARIUS (21 Jan -19 Feb)	Blue Agate	Amethyst	Jacinth
PISCES (20 Feb - 20 Mar)	Amethyst	Aquamarine	Amethyst

Use your Wisdom - the ability to think and act utilising knowledge, experience, understanding, common sense and insight.

According to the teachings of the Holy Quran:

The Universal Life Force, the maker and sustainer of the world, the creator of and provider for man, the Active Force and Effective Power in Nature are all one and the same, known to some as Allah and to others as God. This is the secret of all secrets and the most supreme of all beings.

Belief in God and His great power alone can provide mankind with the best possible explanation of many mysterious things in life. This is the safest way to true knowledge and spiritual insight, the right path to good behaviour and sound morals, the surest guide to happiness and prosperity.

And finally.

In this world of uncertainties you will, as you travel along your journey through life, discover that not everything goes quite according to plan. At these times in our lives it's often reassuring to realise that deep down within the very heart of our souls, we know that there's more to this life than meets the eye, and that reaching out through the mysteries of life we all have our own guides, our angels helping us through. We are part of creation, just as Gemstones and Crystals are. We are all connected to the universe; by looking beyond our world we will in time realise that the things which we seek outside, we already have within.

Gemstones and Crystals are tools to help to connect to that which we desire. It's like making a phone call to a helpline: the Gemstones and Crystals are the phone, we do the dialling and the asking, and then we hope that the Universal Life Force can help. Now dial the number that best suits you.

For further details - write to:
Rosewood
P.O. Box 219, Huddersfield, West Yorkshire. HD2 2YT

E-mail enquiries to: info@rosewood-gifts.co.uk

Or why not visit our website for even more information:

www. rosewood-gifts.co.uk

Change Your Life

By using the most powerful Crystal on earth

By
Robert W. Wood D.Hp
(Diploma in Hypnotherapy)

Rosewood Publishing

BK12

Discovering the most powerful Crystal on earth.

In the world of minerals, the most amazing and most powerful crystal of them all has got to be the Quartz family of crystals. You can find them in quartz watches and at the heart of all computers. They are even used to make the windows and the heat shields for the space shuttles, to enable astronauts to survive the intense heat from re-entry into the earth's atmosphere. The material used for this is called 'fused quartz'. Fused quartz is resistant to heat - very useful if you want to see into hot places. Another example of its use is in windows for furnaces.

The most common element on earth is oxygen, and the second is silicon. The most common of all crystals is silicon quartz, a crystal that grows from the combination of silicon and oxygen. Your computer, either at home or at work, will have in it a 'computer chip' - and it really is a 'chip'; a chip of silicon quartz crystal. That's why they call the home of computer chips, in Los Angeles, 'Silicon Valley'.

The point is that, although you may not have realised it, you are using crystals every day of the week. These crystals, in the form of computer chips, liquid crystal displays, clocking devices, etc, are extensively being used throughout the whole of the telecommunications industry, and are all doing some very important basic things with energy.

They are helping to change, maintain and manipulate the characteristics of energy, so as to perform specific tasks. They can store, amplify, correct and control energy waves.

Not so mysteriously either as it turns out, because it's a natural property of crystals to be able to do all of this. And the emphasis here is on 'natural'.

I can hear you saying: 'So how does knowing all this enable us to change our lives?' Well, it doesn't - not in itself, that is; but what you are about to discover is that 'it takes two to tango'. Have you ever used an epoxy resin glue?

One company advertises that it sets super-strong in minutes and is strong enough to lift a car. The glue comes in two tubes. One's the epoxy and the other the hardener. Neither of them in themselves can do that much, but once the two are mixed together then - wow! This stuff is powerful, and it's all been done naturally by a chemical reaction. Once the two have been mixed together there is no going back. The glue has got to set.

The greatest Crystal of them all
Both carbon and silicon enjoy a special status within chemistry: carbon as an element in organic compounds, and silicon (together with oxygen) as the most important rock-forming element - rock crystal. Silicon is one of the trace elements found in the human body. Trace elements are to be understood as metals, and elements similar to metals, which occur naturally in the body in very tiny concentrations. Most of them are vitally important for man - and here we have a physical connection with crystals

If quartz crystal is the most powerful crystal in the mineral world, then the greatest of them all in the animal kingdom, with all its multiple-combinations of trace elements, has got to be MAN.

Power, without knowledge, is useless.
Do you remember how, in the movie 'Superman', Clark Kent had all the power but not the knowledge? In the early part of the film we see him kicking a football into outer space, and racing a train and winning. His earthly father tells him, 'You are here for a reason.' However, this doesn't help Clark Kent to understand why he is different. But when he turns eighteen he takes a green crystal that was sent along as a teaching aid by his real father, Jor-El, and we see him intuitively travel to the frozen north, where he throws the green crystal and sees a crystalline building rise up from the glaciers. Upon entering the building, Clark finds the green crystal again, and when he places it in the appropriate place on a crystalline control panel, a vision of Jor-El appears and starts to teach him who he is, what he is, where he has come from and why; all about Kryptonian, his home planet, and Kryptonian philosophy.

Acquiring all this knowledge takes Clark twelve years, and we next see him no longer an eighteen-year-old boy, but a thirty-year-old man, with all the confidence and knowledge of who he is. We see an amazingly powerful, confident yet graceful figure take off and fly, and so the real story begins.

By changing the way we think, we can change the future.

It's one thing being told what we can do; but it's another understanding how to do it. Haven't we been told by religious leaders, for thousands of years, to pray? Now if we could understand the power behind the prayer, I am sure more of us would be praying. There are several natural laws of the Universe. These natural laws are exact laws that do not change; they govern all physical and mental sciences. One is the law of cause and effect, and another the law of right thinking. Right thinking starts by recognising the powers of the subconscious mind, the creative power of our thoughts and mental imaginings from within, and how it all works.

You can wish, hope, pray and worry yourself sick until you are a hundred years old. However, if you don't understand the law of right thinking (praying) by using visualisations and **'imagining with feeling'**, you will always be like a ship at sea without stabilisers, just bobbing along, being knocked from pillar to post, having to take life as it comes, believing that nothing you can do can change it. Does this sound anything like your life so far? Wouldn't you prefer to be the ship with the stabilisers? Remember it's the same seas that everybody's travelling on, with calm periods and stormy seasons. This we may not be able to change, but the way we travel, I believe we can. If given the choice, wouldn't you prefer to travel first class and with stabilisers? This book is all about discovering how you can. Take your time, because it takes time.

A journey begins.
In the study of hypnotherapy, you would probably think, like I did, that the hardest part of the course would be 'how to hypnotise someone'. So imagine my surprise to be told that it was both the simplest and the easiest part of the whole course; that the hardest was going to be the understanding beyond the teaching. A little like the difference between knowing how to drive a car and knowing how it's been designed and built.

My intention here, within these writings, is to simply help direct you towards your own understanding of universal law and the law of right thinking.

What's in a number?

How many stars are there? In the Bible it says the stars are as numerous and as countless as the grains of sand on the seashore. However, science has estimated the number to be 10 to the power 21, that is 1 with 21 noughts - and this is what it looks like: 1,000,000,000,000,000,000,000. It's a lot. However, if you take the number of neurones in the brain (these are cells specialised to conduct nerve impulses) you may be surprised to find that there are 10 to the power of 12, that is 12 noughts - look: 1,000,000,000,000. But did you know Albert Einstein said that imagination was more important than knowledge? Here's an example. Who came up with the number 32,768? Was it knowledge or imagination? Scientists discovered that the atoms within a micro-thin slice of synthetic quartz crystal emit a very precise electronic pulse, when power - often from a tiny battery - is passed through it; in fact it vibrates at precisely 32,768 times per second. Now that's knowledge; but let's see what imagination did with this knowledge. Imagination discovered that if you channel the pulses through microchip circuitry, and then successively halve the pulse in a series of 15 steps, then the result is really astounding: it produces a single, constant pulse per second. This is very precise, it's even precise to within a second or two a year, which is why watches and clocks are now so accurate - a uniting of science and the imagination.

The marvel of science

Hundreds of years ago, everyone believed that the Earth was at the centre of the universe. Today we know better, but a complete picture remains elusive. From the ancient notion of a flat Earth to today's theories on the very shape of past and future history, ideas of the universe have evolved with the help of scientific discovery and the eternal human imagination. Plato spoke metaphorically of how male and female are actually the divided halves of one primordial being. Each half, Plato tells us, is looking to the other for its completeness. If we are going to take advantage of our hidden potential, that 'something' we are searching for, it may be useful to understand that the masculine and feminine sides of our psyche must be united. This theme of being united occurs regularly.

It's the 'bringing together of two parts' that often holds the key, including man and crystals.

De-mystifying the mysteries.
Just because you can't see it, doesn't mean it's not there. The power behind birthstones, lucky talismans, charms, amulets and healing crystals is real: be in no doubt. We are talking POWER here, real power. For many years I have given talks entitled 'Discover the Hidden Power in Gemstones' or 'An Evening of Mystery and Imagination'. These talks on birthstones, talismans and healing crystals often include a demonstration on crystal healing, and this has nearly always produced amazing results. Over the years I have spoken to more than a thousand groups, well over one hundred thousand people in all, and I have seen and heard many unusual things.

About half my audiences are church groups, and if I have a gift at all it's being able to take 'church language' and change it into 'new age'. I try to de-mystify the mysteries, explain what may be happening and how, whilst trying to be non-judgmental. On page 18 you'll see a list of my books, written on the many subjects of birthstones, talismans and healing crystals. Within my talks there comes a point where I say, 'Either the stones work for you, or they don't.' If you win at bingo regularly and you are using a lucky bingo stone (a talisman), then you're more likely to believe in them. It's the same with healing crystals: if they have worked for you, then you'll believe. However, according to holistic healers, when we are ill we are 'out of balance' with nature, and a crystal can help us to return back 'into balance', to good health. It's a little like when a radio station goes off station; we tune it back in, back 'into balance'. If we take the view that all this is somehow God-given, that it's the law of the universal life force and is found within the mind, then I believe within these writings you can become so empowered by discovering for yourself a code that will enable you to change your life, and that includes your health, luck and even the future.

Beginning the search.
Each one of us is responsible for our own search, a search for meaning and the choices we make, but it's worth remembering that seeking and enquiring can only have one purpose: that is, to find; and once we have found, then this stage of the journey, the search, is completed.

"There are many gates into the garden of heaven", the Sufi masters say, "but to enter the garden you need only pass through one."

The challenge is to find the right one and the right guidance. It's not easy in a world where religion can easily be transformed into inquisition, and the urge to save souls into holy wars. A way is wrong when it can harm, deceive or mislead you. All journeys start at the beginning. The fact that you are reading this book shows your intention to discover more, and the best way will be to discover for yourself those parts within us that are able to connect with the Supreme Principles of the universe. Within every human psyche there exist higher mental and emotional centres capable of unimaginable states of awareness, unless they are awakened by proper guidance, then it's likened to living your life out in the basement of a thousand roomed palace.

Mind over matter?
Can you ride a bike, or use a typewriter? Can you swim or drive a car? If the answer to any of these questions is 'yes', then you have already experienced your greatest asset from within your mind. Let me explain: there are two main parts to our brains, the conscious and subconscious. The conscious acts like a gatekeeper for the mind and has the power to direct - it's how we think; but it's the subconscious that performs the tasks. Like driving a car - you decide where you're going consciously, but it's the subconscious that does all the driving. It's as if within any skill there's a kind of 'knowing', and life becomes much more comfortable when that 'knowing' kicks in.

There are pictures that can show this effect quite clearly - for example, this shifting staircase. When you first look, you may see the staircase as if you were standing at the bottom right hand corner of the picture, ready to walk up the steps. Then it will change, almost as if by magic, so that you are now in the bottom left hand corner, underneath the steps - or vice versa.

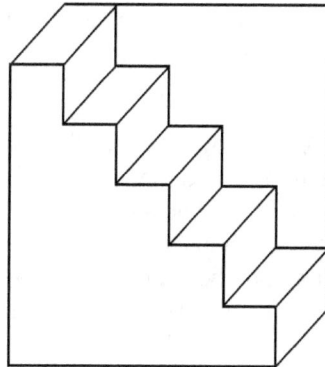

197

This picture is a way of revealing the subconscious, because there are two ways you can see this picture. Consciously you see it one way, but within a few seconds your subconscious sees another way of interpreting it and has to show the alternative to you, and then the picture will start to fluctuate backwards and forwards.

Think of the mind like Concorde, the supersonic plane. The pilot represents the conscious, while the subconscious is represented by the plane, the engineers who built it, the scientists that helped, the aviation authorities that allow it to fly, the ground crews including air traffic control that support it. The responsibility is with the captain - but just imagine the size of the support team. Wow! It's colossal. With the power we have within us, is it possible that minds can move matter? The answer is yes! It really can. Read my book 'Discover Why Crystal Healing Works', where I explain how I moved a mountain; or read my book on crystal dowsing. For a more everyday example, think of stomach ulcers. It's a fact that these are brought about because of the way we think, mainly due to stress and anxiety. The surgeon can repair the ulcer, but not the cause that created it.

The power of the mind.
One of the most amazing stories I ever heard was about a very wealthy woman, in her late fifties, who went for hypnotherapy. During the preliminary interview she was asked if she had ever had children. Her reply was that sadly her only regret in life was that she never had, although she had spent most of her life 'leaving no stone unturned', including consulting one of the best and most expensive gynaecologists in Harley Street.

This story I know will be difficult to believe, but it is true. During her consultations it became apparent that she had in fact in her late teens been pregnant and had had a miscarriage very late on into the pregnancy. I won't go into the details here, but the experience had been so devastatingly traumatic that her mind, the conscious mind, decided to conceal the memory from her. This can often happen after a bad car accident. Can you imagine the woman's surprise, the shock and horror when her memory decided to reveal this amazing truth about her past? It's really very rare to find such an extreme case, but this story goes on to provide an even more amazing revelation of the power within the mind.

Before I tell you more I think it best if I explain a little about the power of hypnotherapy.

Hypnotherapy.

It seems to have started with 'The Psychology of the Unconscious', published in 1911 by the Swiss psychiatrist Carl Jung (1875-1961). Jung (pronounced 'Young') was the leading collaborator of Sigmund Freud (1856-1939). Jung's research into psychoanalysis led him to disagree with Freud's interpretations. Sigmund Freud, the founder of modern psychology, discovered in 1895 that he was able to cure a patient of hysteria. Her illness was characterised by emotional outbursts and some physical symptoms, and Freud cured her by allowing her to talk freely whilst under hypnosis. Later, finding hypnosis inadequate, Freud encouraged patients just to ramble on with their thoughts; whilst in a state of relaxed consciousness. This method of drawing memories from the subconscious to the conscious mind became known as 'psychoanalysis'.

A huge difference between psychotherapy and hypnotherapy is down to timescale. Whereas psychotherapy, psychoanalysis or counselling may take one hundred hours to complete, in hypnotherapy it can take less than ten. Hypnosis speeds up the process. This type of hypnosis is certainly not like that induced by a stage hypnotist; it's more of a state of relaxed consciousness. The patient is always consciously awake.

The last resort.

Who would see a hypnotherapist? Just about anybody who has found the medical profession unable to find anything wrong, implying that their illness is psychosomatic - it's probably all in the mind. What you are discovering is just how powerful the mind is. People know when there's something wrong. Some describe it as a 'gut feeling'. Things are just not right.

Here's a rule of thumb: if everybody says, 'You're fine; you look OK; pull yourself together, there's nothing wrong,' and you know deep down that there is, then see a hypnotherapist. If you are suffering from anything that could be described as an irrational fear or phobia - for example, being scared of wasps, bees, blood, closed-in places or open spaces, or if you dare not fly but would like to - then see a hypnotherapist.

They can really help. However, if everybody is telling you that there's something wrong with you and you don't think there is, then see a psychiatrist - you're probably ill.

Back to Freud.
The disagreement between Freud and Carl Jung stemmed from Freud's method of 'letting sleeping dogs lie' - in other words, what's in the past should be left in the past. Jung thought that this was the cause of all the problems later on in life. He believed that if the 'suppressed memories', as he called them, were drawn from the subconscious and brought into the conscious, the adult would be able to handle them. And the amazing thing is, he was right; once the thought or memory has been brought into the adult's conscious world, all the irrational fears and phobias just disappear for ever. The process is described by many as being 'let out of prison', 'feeling free', or 'like having a bad tooth pulled out' - it's such a relief.

The power of mind over matter.
To go back to our story of the woman who had had a miscarriage: her hypnotherapy sessions were drawn to a very successful conclusion, all repressed memories were found - a very satisfactory result. About a year later she wrote to say that she had seen her gynaecologist and had been given some surprising news. She explained that she had been unable to have children because she had had a retroverted womb (her uterus was turned backwards); but she had now been told that for some inexplicable reason it had just righted itself and was now normal. Can you see a connection? If something like a suppressed memory can have such a devastating effect as to tilt her womb, what could you do, knowing how it all works. There are thousands of such stories of 'miracles'; they're happening all around us all the time.

Failure and success are not accidents or incidents,
they are influenced by a state of mind.

Psychic energy.
Where do you get your energy from: introversion or extroversion? To give you an idea: imagine two friends who both teach in a school. After a full day's work one of them regularly goes and plays badminton whilst the other just wants to get home and spend a little time on their own.

Now if you were the one going home tired, then you could be forgiven for thinking that there was something wrong with you, especially when your friend seems to have so much energy.

There are only two ways of acquiring psychic energy: you create it either from within - called 'introversion' - or from without - 'extroversion'. The extrovert, after a full day at school, has overcharged their batteries and needs to discharge, whilst the introvert needs to re-energise within themselves. In other words, the extrovert is drawing energy from the people around them, and the introvert is having their energy taken away from them, hence the expression 'feeling drained'. If you locked up an extrovert into solitary confinement it would probably kill them, whereas the introvert would love it. These are two extremes, but you may recognise yourself from the descriptions.

The collective unconscious.
According to Jung, the personal subconscious contains lost memories, painful ideas that are repressed. But he also identified what he called a 'collective unconscious', an extension of the personal subconscious. He believed that at this level of mind family, social groups, nations and even all humanity were connected. Imagine what he is saying: that each one of us has access to a collective subconscious. Just like the Internet, we can, through our minds, somehow connect to all of humanity. We can ask for help and know that the thought is being picked up on. As owners of our minds, our job is to make sure we are being heard. Discovering this code is mind-blowing.

You only have to ask.
It takes no more effort to aim high in life, to demand your share of good fortune, to be healthy, to have peace of mind, than it does to accept misery, ill health and poverty. Through these lines a poet correctly touched this universal truth:

> I bargained with life for a penny
> and life would pay no more,
> however I begged at evening
> when I counted my scanty store.

201

For life is a just employer,
he gives you what you ask;
but once you have set the wages,
why, you must bear the task.

I worked for a menial's hire,
only to learn, dismayed,
that any wage I had asked of life
life would have willingly paid.

A motivational book.

I read these words one afternoon whilst in Wales on a business trip. I don't
know why, but for some reason someone staying in the same hotel the
previous night had giving me a book by Napoleon Hill called 'Think and
Grow Rich', a classic motivational book sharing a philosophy for
achievement. I can highly recommend the book. I had some time to spare
and so I read it, and the words that day seemed to be speaking to me. One
of the principles was that everybody has an edge. It may be only a little
thing but nevertheless we all have this edge, and the writer seemed to be
saying that if we use our minds we can turn our dreams into reality - by
using the right way of thinking.

It seemed to make sense, and so I tried it. You'll have to read my book
'Discover Why Crystal Healing Works" for more details, but looking back
I can't believe the changes in my life. Not all were good, but it's strange
how even the not-so-good have turned out for the better. I moved from a
three-bedroomed semi into a four-bedroomed detached; from a salesman
to a managing director, from driving an old Astra to a new Volvo 740 with
built-in car phone.

A chance of a new life now awaits you. You only have to reach out and
take it. But remember that it's you yourself who must do the reaching.
One of the greatest gifts on earth can be found within the mind. Once we
are seriously involved in researching this, it's best to be prepared and well
versed in the rules. It's the Law of Right Thinking.

Can any good come from a lie?

The answer is 'yes, if the intention is well meant'. We live our lives in the conscious world but carry with us a support pack like nothing else on earth. How it's been designed, or evolved, still remains a mystery - but not the fact that we have it. The conscious is likened to an iceberg: you can only see the tip of it, nine-tenths is below the water level. And it's the same with the mind: the bulk of it you can't see, but you can easily experience it.

Have you ever seen a stage hypnotist when he gets people to do strange and outrageous things? If you think you could never do these things, think again - because we all do, in our dreams. This is why the mind can be dangerous. If you want to know how dangerous, imagine a child running the world from a computer console. That's your subconscious; and that's why the conscious has got to be in charge.

The placebo effect.

Do you know what a placebo is? It's an inactive substance, like a sugar pill, given to a patient who insists on receiving medication, or when someone, maybe a doctor or psychologist, believes that a patient would benefit from the psychological deception of believing they have been given medication. It really is well known in the medical profession.

However, here is an amazing fact. Although it's based on a lie - someone being told that the 'medicine' they are taking will cure them - the surprise is that it actually does. How can it? And the answer is, we don't fully know. Just like we don't know what electricity is - but that doesn't stop us using it. Early man didn't know what a magnet was, but that didn't stop him circumnavigating the world using it. Today we call it a compass.

It's thought that for some, the belief that the placebo will work is enough to trigger something within the mind that reacts with the body to bring about a positive result. These are not isolated cases, in fact they are so common that whenever they are testing new drugs they do what are called 'blind clinical tests', whereby half the patients are given the proper medicine and the others the placebo. It's an attempt to show how effective the drugs really are. What would you do if you knew how this worked, and that you could use this placebo effect to your advantage!

How to change the future.

Change the way you think and you can change your future. Science may be able now to give an explanation of how all this may work. We are standing at the very edge of a staggering, unimaginable advance in science and technology. Science for the very first time can see into a whole new dimension of reality with the discovery of 'SCALAR' electromagnetic wave technology. It is through this branch of science that we will be able to cast more light on the potential capabilities of minerals, gems and crystals and their interaction with man.

Imagine you have a powerful hand-held magnet. As you come closer to a metal object, there is a moment when the metal object jumps at speed towards the magnet. Science seems to have found a way of harnessing this energy and converting it into electricity, and this electricity will be free. This new knowledge seems to be able for the first time to explain how crystals and gems are able to interact with humans. It's a major breakthrough.

The Law of Belief.
When you begin to use the 'magic' power of your subconscious, then you'll notice small miracles happening around you, and more will come. What do you believe? Because maybe it's not the thing believed in, but the belief itself that brings the results. The law of belief works in all the religions around the world. Buddhist, Hindu, Christian, Moslem and Hebrew all may get some answers through their prayers. Not because of a particular creed, ritual or ceremony, but through belief. The law of life is the law of belief, and belief could be summed up briefly as a thought in the mind.

As a man thinks, feels and believes, so is the condition of his mind, body and circumstances. A technique or methodology based on an understanding of what you are doing and why you are doing it will help you to bring about a successful result, a realisation of your heart's desire.

The great secret possessed by the great men of all ages was their ability to contact and release the powers of their subconscious mind.

Visualisation
The easiest and most obvious way to formulate an idea is to visualise it, imagine it in your 'mind's eye', and see it as if it's real.

You can see through your eyes what already exists in the outer world, and in a similar way, that which you can imagine and visualise in your mind's eye exists in the invisible realms of the mind. The idea, the thought in the form of your imagination is the substance of things hoped for and the evidence of things to come. The Chinese say, 'A picture is worth a thousand words'. William James, the father of American psychology, stressed the fact that the subconscious mind will bring about any picture held in the mind and backed by feeling and a belief.

Use your Imagination, and not willpower.
When using your subconscious mind you are able to imagine without the interference of any opponent - mainly the intellect, which can be your worst enemy, especially if it decides to be negative. Neither can you use willpower. You will find your intellect trying to get in the way, but persist in maintaining a simple, childlike, miracle-making faith.

The Bible says, 'Therefore I tell you, whatever you ask for in prayer, believe that you have received it, and it will be yours'. How do you believe you have received something? You imagine you already have it. But here is the secret, here is the code: you have to do it with a feeling or with an emotion. For example, if you want to become pregnant then make sure you have a fertility stone like a moonstone; it helps to focus the mind. Now imagine the desired effect, for example a doctor saying, 'Congratulations, you're expecting,' but imagine at the same time how would you feel if that happened. Energise the thought you are bringing from the future into the present, and when you can, the whole of universal law will be at your disposal.

More examples.
You're ill and worried. Get a healing stone (a rose quartz is quite good), quieten the mind, then visualise a friend or someone in the family saying, "You're looking well," and you replying, "I feel great." Even if you feel terrible, that doesn't matter - remember the placebo effect. It's based on a lie. Or, have you got a bad memory? If you have, you can improve it tenfold by not admitting it and in fact by going the other way and repeating, 'I have a good memory, my memory's brilliant, I have total recall.' The fact that you may not is immaterial. The subconscious believes whatever you tell it; this is what a hypnotist relies on. If you want a new

job and you have an interview - then get a stone for good luck, or if you're feeling anxious a stone to relax with. Quieten the mind, relax, then imagine it's now after the interview, someone is asking you how it went, and you say something like, "You won't believe this but I got the job!"

Then imagine at the same time how would you feel if you had. Get excited, punch the air, remember you've just got the job.

It's imagining a feeling that most people have trouble with. For example, imagine you got into a taxi and gave half a dozen different directions to the driver in the first few minutes of the journey. He would become hopelessly confused and probably would refuse to go anywhere. It's the same when working with your subconscious mind. There must be a clear-cut image in your mind - your visualisation - and it must have the one ingredient that is necessary for universal law to become activated: a feeling, an emotion. Given half a chance, who wouldn't want to be a millionaire? But would you know how it feels to be a millionaire? Get into the part, imagine how it would feel; the rewards are staggering.

An inner child workshop.
In July 1991 I attended a five-day 'inner child' workshop at a retreat in Surrey. It was organised by the 'Sisters of the Cenacle', an international congregation ministering to both men and women of all faiths. The name Cenacle refers to the room where the last supper was celebrated and the Holy Spirit descended onto the apostles. The event was advertised as a workshop to explore the connections between childhood woundedness and areas of adult life. It was run by two sisters, one I believe was well known to the Queen Mum and the other had been to universities in America as part of her studies within the church. They were both very knowledgeable. I thought they were like the Jesuit priests.

At the time I was studying to become a hypnotherapist and thought that this workshop could help me to understand some of my studies. These types of courses are never to be taken lightly, but imagine my surprise when I received a letter, telling me that I had been accepted but going on to say, *'I should like to point out that if you do not have a follow-up support system for yourself, e.g. a counsellor or spiritual director, then the two sisters running the course are not able to accept responsibility for anything which may be surfaced during the workshop.*

Nor, given the demanding and intense nature of the workshop, will they be able to give extra time for support during it.

'I would urge you, therefore, to reflect carefully as to whether you still wish to attend the workshop.'

Wow! What a build-up - and I wasn't disappointed. Here is the point of the story: about thirty-five of us had been meditating for nearly two days and I felt it just wasn't touching me; I was expecting more. (I did get more, but not until later on in the week.) I caught one of the sisters and told her how I felt, and she said, "It's because you are already there, Robert. You and three others, you are already where all the others are wanting to be." She went on to say something quite astounding: "You can achieve more in a three-minute prayer than most can in hours." Well, did that give me something to think about! It turned out to be this technique of visualising and imaging with feeling.

The principal reasons for failure are lack of confidence and too much effort. Many people block answers to their prayers by failing to fully understand the workings of the mind. When you know how your mind works, you become more confident. When you imagine the reality of the fulfilled desire and can feel the thrill of its accomplishment, your subconscious mind is activated to bring about the realisation of your dreams, your goals, your desire.

Psalm 19:14.
Maybe this is what the Psalmist really meant when he wrote: **'May the words of my mouth** (our thoughts, mental images and the good) **and the meditations of my heart** (our nature, our feelings and emotions) **be pleasing in thy sight, O Lord** (the law of right thinking of the subconscious mind) **my rock, and my redeemer** (it's the power and wisdom of our subconscious mind that can redeem us from sickness, poverty and misery).

Within each of us is a kind of personalised instruction book revealing where we have come from, where we are going and who we really are. Somehow, in each human there is, deep within the psyche, a knowledge of everything connecting with the universe. It's as if there's a veil that conceals it all. Just as the sun is always shining behind the clouds, waiting to break through, so universal life force waits for our psychological clouds to part. Maybe no one book, prophet or religion possesses the whole and absolute truth, but a value can be found in each and all of them.

What we can choose, especially as we increase in wisdom and years, is the way we approach the circumstances of our lives. Don't we all believe that what we see around us when we walk down the street is an accurate reflection of what really is? What we don't realise is the innumerable forms of energy surrounding us at any given moment. These range from radio signals and light waves to radiation, electricity and magnetism - not to mention our own inner electrical and chemical discharges, our thoughts, senses, feelings and emotions, and so it goes on and on. Discover how to use all this energy by harnessing it; it's all around us.

To summarise: -
From just two common elements, the king and queen of the mineral world, comes Quartz Crystal, a crystal befitting any crown jewels. However, the most amazing and powerful crystal of them all is **MAN**. Where can we find the power to change our lives? It's in the 'Law of Right Thinking'; it's found in the mind.

There are two main parts to the mind, the conscious and the subconscious, and both must be in harmony. Where is the power, then? It's in the mind. Where in the mind? In the subconscious; you can see it at work with the picture of the staircase. But where is it in the subconscious? It's in the Imagination. So how can I activate this power? You must imagine your desired effect or goal; your dream. See them in your mind's eye. Then imagine how would you feel if you achieved it. Energise the thought by adding a feeling. It's called, by some, a 'scientific prayer'. The role of the crystal could be similar to that of a booster station, to help increase the power and relay the message. Just like the mobile phone masts you can see everywhere; they are there to boost the signals.

And finally ...
... on a personal note: In 1986 I sent away for a booklet entitled 'Power for Living'. A package arrived; I opened it, and it wasn't what I expected. However, I did get chance to read it and I found it to be interesting. It was religious and I wasn't. It concluded with a prayer, and I repeated it and signed it to acknowledge that I had read it. Next came a kaleidoscope of emotions and feelings, experiences lasting over an 18-month period.

I listened, I studied and I observed. I now write books and give talks on the subject of the mysteries surrounding Gemstones and Crystals.

I have found that the very understanding I discovered in church can also be found outside church. It's in all religions - Christianity, Islam, Judaism, Hinduism, Buddhism etc, even in atheism and agnosticism - and in all walks of life. A tiny minority have said I can't be a Christian because of my views. How nice then, to see the new Archbishop of Canterbury, Dr. Rowan Williams, being admitted to the highest order of Druids; to see the Queen, the head of the Church of England, going into a Moslem mosque and a Hindu and Sikh temple during her Golden Jubilee year.

When people ask, I reply that I am a follower of Jesus Christ and his teachings; and if that makes me a Christian then that's what I am. Read what Jesus said about people who think differently:

"Master," said John, "we saw a man driving out demons in your name and we tried to stop him because he is not one of us." "Do not stop him," Jesus said, "for whoever is not against you is for you.".
Luke 9 - 49.

Very early on in my search, I was given a 'mission'. I didn't understand it at the time, but it was this: "De-mystify the mysteries". This thought over the years has become all-consuming. These writings are part of that mission. Life is a journey. Live the journey; discover your way, because, for you, your way is the right way.

Whatever has happened in your life up until now, whatever you may have dreamed of, believed in or hoped for, remember it's all now in the past and can't be changed, however hard you wish it could. A new life, a new chance and a new hope now awaits you. But you yourself must take the first step and do the reaching. What was it that Spock used to say? - "Live long and prosper". I couldn't agree more.

Rosewood
P.O. Box 219, Huddersfield, West Yorkshire. HD2 2YT
E-mail enquiries to: info@rosewood-gifts.co.uk

Or why not visit our website for more information:
www. rosewood-gifts.co.uk

INDEX

'An Alternative View on
Crystal Healing'
Revealing "power for Life's" Secret Ingredient

A book intended to help and guide those who are interested in alternative treatments. Treatments without the side-effects that drugs can have. The information is in direct response to those that would like to know more and is part of our series of books called 'Power for Life'. Books based on and around the mysteries surrounding gemstones and crystals.

Here you will find information about the Metaphysical, Astrological and Physical properties of Gemstones and Crystals.

Including a glossary of gemstones & Crystal

I believe that each and every one of us, irrespective of colour, creed or religion, is empowered with an energy. A power that is so awesome, that once triggered, it can heal, change your luck, even 'move mountains'.

Read my story of how I moved a mountain
by using this "Power for Life's" secret ingredient.

ISBN 978-0-9567913-2-0

Welcome to the world of Rosewood Gifts/Publishing

If you like natural products, hand-crafted gifts
Including Gemstone Jewellery, objects of natural
Beauty – the finest examples from Mother Nature, tinged
With an air of Mystery – then we hope you will not be disappointed.
For those who can enjoy that feeling of connection with the
Esoteric nature of Gemstones and Crystals, then our 'Themed'
"Power for Life" – Power Bracelets could be ideal for you.

We regularly give inspirational "Power for Life" seminars

**These are presented by Robert W. Wood D.Hp
For like minds wanting to find peace and Harmony in
Mind, Body and Spirit.**

A captivating story about the world's fascination with natural
Gemstones and Crystals, often described as both intriguing
and electrifying,
but never disappointing.

To see our full range of books, jewellery and gifts

Visit our web site – www.rosewood-gifts.co.uk

To see our latest videos go to 'You Tube'
And type in Rosewood Gifts.

www.ingramcontent.com/pod-product-compliance
Lightning Source LLC
LaVergne TN
LVHW051512080426
835509LV00017B/2037